Land Reform in Brazil: The Management of Social Change

Marta Cehelsky

Westview Press / Boulder, Colorado

Copyright © 1979 by Westview Press, Inc.

Published in 1979 in the United States of America by
     Westview Press, Inc.
     5500 Central Avenue
     Boulder, Colorado 80301
     Frederick A. Praeger, Publisher

Library of Congress Catalog Card Number: 79-3974
ISBN: 0-89158-075-1

Printed and bound in the United States of America

To Michael R. and Irene Cehelsky

Land Reform in Brazil

Westview Replica Editions

This book is a Westview Replica Edition. The concept of
Replica Editions is a response to the crisis in academic and
informational publishing. Library budgets for books have been
severely curtailed; economic pressures on the university presses
and the few private publishing companies primarily interested in
scholarly manuscripts have severely limited the capacity of the
industry to properly serve the academic and research communities.
Many manuscripts dealing with important subjects, often representing the highest level of scholarship, are today not economically viable publishing projects. Or, if they are accepted for
publication, they are often subject to lead times ranging from
one to three years. Scholars are understandably frustrated when
they realize that their first-class research cannot be published
within a reasonable time frame, if at all.

Westview Replica Editions are our practical solution to the
problem. The concept is simple. We accept a manuscript in camera-
ready form and move it immediately into the production process.
The responsibility for textual and copy editing lies with the
author or sponsoring organization. If necessary we will advise
the author on proper preparation of footnotes and bibliography.
We prefer that the manuscript be typed according to our speci-
fications, though it may be acceptable as typed for a dissertation or prepared in some other clearly organized and readable
way. The end result is a book produced by lithography and bound
in hard covers. Initial edition sizes range from 400 to 600
copies, and a number of recent Replicas are already in second
printings. We include among Westview Replica Editions only works
of outstanding scholarly quality or of great informational value,
and we will continue to exercise our usual editorial standards
and quality control.

Land Reform in Brazil:
The Management of Social Change

Marta Cehelsky

Land reform stands as one of the most explosive issues in modern Brazil. Having contributed to the downfall of João Goulart's populist democracy and to the establishment of an authoritarian regime, it became, ironically, an early major policy objective of the new military government.

This volume documents the disintegration of Brazilian democracy and identifies the major reasons for its instability and its tendency to revert to authoritarian rule. Dr. Cehelsky explores the significance and treatment of land reform under democratic and authoritarian rule and assesses the overall impact of a measure originally intended to produce social reform. Viewed analytically, the management of the land reform issue in Brazil attests to the resilience of the traditional elites and their power to determine substantially the nature and rate of accommodation of social and economic change.

Marta Cehelsky is a policy analyst at NASA. She has taught political science at Brooklyn College and the University of Houston and has served as advisor to the commissioner of the U.S. Immigration and Naturalization Service.

Contents

Tables and Figures

Figure

Preface

Throughout this book, Brazilian terms are frequently used in preference to imperfect English translations, or lengthy explanations. A glossary of such terms is provided for ready reference. Likewise, I adhere to the Brazilian custom of using first names or cognomen interchangeably with or in preference to family names. Thus, João Goulart is frequently referred to as Jango; Jânio Quadros as Jânio, etc. Also in keeping with common Brazilian usage, I refer to the overthrow of the Goulart administration in 1964 as the "revolution." This usage is a convenience and does not constitute a judgment of the true character of the event.

This book is a milestone in a Brazilian odyssey which began in senior year at Barnard College. Beginning with my senior thesis on the modern Brazilian presidency, observing and analyzing Brazilian politics -- its institutions, development, and leadership -- has been a source of constant fascination. Ronald Schnedier helped me take those first steps into the study of Brazil. For this and for his readiness over the years to share his extraordinary grasp and detailed knowledge of Brazilian politics and offer constant encouragement I owe him special gratitude.

In the course of preparing this book, I have
benefitted from the help, advice, discussions, and
critiques of many people. My largest debt is to the
many Brazilians who have made it possible for me to
study the politics of their country and share their
insights. I promised confidentiality and anonymity
to all individuals I interviewed, and therefore do
not list them in the bibliography.

Sergio Bertoni, director of the cadastral department of the now defunct Brazilian Institute of
Agrarian Reform, lent invaluable assistant in providing access to studies and documents prepared by his
organization. José Felice, director of the gaucho
branch of the Institute, did the same in Rio Grande
do Sul. Amaro Cavalcanti and Ben Hur Raposo of the
National Confederation of Agriculture provided documents and records on the activities of the CNA.
Edgar Teixeira Leite, also an official of the CNA,
generously opened up his personal library to me.
General Golbery de Couto e Silva provided access to
the archives of IPES, the Institute of Social Studies
and Research. Manuel Diegues Júnior kindly helped
with materials on rural problems in Brazil in the
Centro Latino Americano de Pesquisas em Ciências
Sociais.

Many of the sources I used for tracing the
political debate on land reform are located in the
Biblioteca Nacional, and in the library of the
Fundação Getúlio Vargas. But special thanks for help
in tracking down valuable sources and documents go
to Roberto de Oliveria Campos, Paulo Assis Ribeiro,
Raymundo Padilha, Assis Badra, João Cleofas, João
Caruso, Thomas Pompeu Accioly Borges, and Aurélio
Viana.

A grant from the Foreign Area Fellowship Program enabled me to research this project in Brazil. In the course of the research effort, I benefitted from discussions and helpful recommendations from Octavio Ianni, Gabriel Cohn, Juarez Rubens Brandão Lopez, Hélio Jaguaribe, Cândido Mendes de Almedia, Lauro Rangel, Philippe Schmitter, Kenneth Erickson, Anthony Leeds, Richard Graham, and Jonathan Dill. Alan Sager and Thomas Louis offered help on the processing of the debates in the Chamber of Deputies and Richard Moore helped with the coding.

Earlier drafts of this manuscript benefitted considerably from the thoughtful criticism of Dankwart Rustow, Douglas Chalmers, and Philip B. Taylor. To Doug Chalmers, and particularly to Dan Rustow, my intellectual debt extends well beyond the subject of this book.

Many have helped and contributed, often unknowingly, to this study, for which, of course, I bear final responsibility. No one, however, has borne the burden of it more or deserves more thanks than David T. Garza, my husband. He has been a fellow researcher, forum and critic for my ideas, and friend. Through many drafts he has provided unflagging moral support, the benefit of his insightful grasp of Brazilian politics and developmental problems, his keen editorial eye, and above all, his patience and sense of humor.

Finally, I thank Virginia Lyerly for her patience and dedication in the frequently trying task of putting this manuscript into its final typed form.

1. Introduction

This is a study of the struggle over land reform policy in Brazil during the 1960s. Its primary
purpose is to provide insight into the workings of
the Brazilian political system in general and the
policy process in particular at a time when Brazil
was undergoing a major crisis of regime. In this
sense, this volume is not so much a study of agriculture and agrarian reform as it is a policy analysis in which land reform functions as an especially
sensitive lens through which the workings of the
political system can be examined. For this reason,
matters such as rural social conditions and agricultural productivity are touched on only tangentially
and for the limited purpose of providing a backdrop
against which the agrarian struggle developed. Similarly, although the treatment of rural social structure and movements is more detailed, its primary
purpose is to enhance our understanding of the impact of social actors on the policy process. Consequently, this is not primarily a study of peasant
movements, or even, in any explicit sense, of rural
development and politicization, although both have an
important bearing on the issue. Discussion of the
nature and significance of the Land Statute which was
ultimately enacted by the military government in

1964, is undertaken more to assess its impact on the
political system and on the distribution of power,
rather than on rural development.

Still, the choice of agriculture as the focus
of this study is not coincidental or casual, either
from the perspective of the evolution of the Brazilian political order, or the crisis and upheaval of
1964 which terminated Brazilian democracy and replaced it with a military regime. Agriculture was
the foundation of the Brazilian economy during colonial and early independence periods, and continues
to be an important element of the economy, although
the industrial sector has come to play an increasingly prominent role. Planter elites have occupied a
central place in the traditional Brazilian political
system, exercised considerable influence in that
system, and contributed crucially to its stability,
survival, and evolution. The modernizing transformation which began roughly in 1930 heralded Brazil's
transition from an agrarian patrimonial political
order to a modern authoritarian state. The revolution of 1964, in which the agrarian controversy played a prominent role, symbolized the initiation of the
final phase of this transformation and centered on
what Barrington Moore and others have indicated as
the gravest of the modernizing hurdles -- that of
incorporating the rural masses into the modern economy and political order.[1]

It is the specific intention of this study to
place the examination of the land reform controversy
in this broad political context and to offer some insight into the systemic importance of the issue.
Although a central purpose of this volume is the reconstruction of the decision on land reform for the

2

1962-1970 period, the analysis is not restricted to
the recreation of the major acts and scenarios of
this agrarian policy drama, or to the recollection
of memorable lines. Rather, the clarification of the
policy mechanism, like a period piece, must be understood in relationship to the dynamics of the historical moment within which it is located and shaped.
In addition to deriving its significance from this
moment by throwing critical decisions and relationships into high relief, such analysis illuminates
the context itself and lends it greater coherence.
Also, since a policy decision contains not only the
elements of a moral drama but also the possibilities
of tragedy, its full appreciation is enhanced by dis-
covering the historical roots of the event and its
characters, and by locating the event itself within
a meaningful developmental framework.

In relating the case study to historical roots,
this volume attempts to provide some insight into the
fundamental continuity of Brazil's political experience. To this end, the argument advanced in the succeeding pages goes beyond the observations of some
recent writings which trace Brazil's current political institutions to Vargas' Estado Nôvo some thirty
years earlier.[2] While acknowledging the importance
of the Vargas dictatorship for the development of
political institutions, this study holds that there
exists a far older traditional basis for the current
institutional structure. Its specific characteristics were evident during the imperial period of early
independence, and its origins rooted in the colonial
era.[3] Despite the considerable impact of modernization, democratic ideologies, and political experimen-
tation over time, Brazil has not yet undergone an

experience basically transforming the traditional
and authoritarian nature of its political order, or
the primary institutional arrangements on which its
has rested.

MODERNIZING AUTHORITARIANISM

This line of investigation is intended to shed
additional light on a type of political system only
recently singled out as worthy of independent study
-- the authoritarian regime. In the 1960s, social
scientific models of development, whether political
or economic in emphasis, were predominently based on
assumptions derived from the experiences of industrial, capitalist democracies. With these schemes,
western scholars hoped to explain, and in some instances guide, the complex developmental processes of
newly modernizing post-colonial nations. Totalitar-
ian, or as I prefer to call them, collectivist state
hegemonic regimes, the revolutionary progeny of developmental failures (it was assumed), were viewed
as the major alternative to the western democratic
tradition. With few exceptions, comparative developmental theorists paid relatively little attention to
the distinct modernizing experience of older, traditional authoritarian systems. A strong assumption
prevailed of their inherent instability and inability to manage and survive crises of economic and social change.

As these assumptions have failed to be borne
out, scholars have begun to study more closely the
persistent phenomenon of stable, authoritarian political orders.[4] Latin American nations and Spain and
Portugal have become particularly important foci of

4

interest for the study of authoritarian regimes and the process by which they undergo industrialization without sacrificing their traditional structures or institutions or succumbing to revolution.

Our theoretical understanding of these regimes, however, remains minimal. As Juan Linz has observed, we relegate them to a "residual" category.[5] The general recognition that conservative authoritarian regimes constitute a stable category apart from others has not automatically resulted in a definition of systemic traits shared by these nations. Furthermore, this lack of analytical clarity has occasioned some confusion as to which regimes fall into the residual category and how far. Linz, for example, suggests that Brazil, a major focal point for study of authoritarian politics, does not constitute an authoritarian regime, but an authoritarian "situation."[6] However, once one recognizes that a certain amount of political instability is characteristic of authoritarian regimes, it remains unclear why Brazilian authoritarianism, with a tradition at least 250 years old, is more situational than, for example, that of Spain, which is now undergoing a "democratic" renaissance.

Unquestionably, a great deal more work needs to be done on authoritarian systems, relating detailed empirical research to theoretical analysis. Not enough is understood about how economic modernization is managed by traditional institutions which, despite extensive social change, maintain a stratified access to the political process and concentration of power in the hands of the state. In particular, there is insufficient insight into the relationship of day to day decision making to the maintenance and continuity

5

of the political order. For example, despite the
fact that the general literature on Brazil is abundant and that in recent yers a number of studies
have appered focusing on Brazilian authoritarianism
and corporatism, detailed issue oriented case studies
of policy and decision making are few.[7] Furthermore,
for the most part, these studies do not explore the
larger theoretical implications of their findings or
place the issues they discuss in a developmental
perspective. Consequently, comparability based on a
common frame of reference is reduced, and theoretical
implications must often be inferred.

Of the three recent major case study approaches,
only one, for instance, that of Nathaniel Leff, makes
an explicit attempt to provide a comprehensive theoretical explanation of the nature of the Brazilian
decision making process.[8] His provocative review of
economic decision making within four issue areas from
1947 to 1964 emphasizes executive discretion and
autonomy in the policy process, and the powerlessness
of traditional elites against the executive technocrats. He attributes the rational, independent role
of the executive to a combination of clientelistic
political organization and a political consensus
akin to Rousseau's general will.[9] In his view, class
and interest group analyses, which attribute considerable. political power to economic groups, are in-
applicable to the Brazilian situation.[10] In the
absence of a powerful interest framework, the executive is apparently in a position to effect a number
of rational, innovative policy decisions even when
they are unpopular with particular economic and social sectors.

Unfortunately, although Leff's analysis offers
some interesting insights into economic decision making for the 1947-1964 period, several weaknesses
limit the general validity of its observations on the
relationship of decision making to the social and
political order. For one thing, President João
Goulart (1961-1964) clearly did not fit the description of the powerful executive unhampered by social
and political considerations in the formulation of
policy. Second, Leff's description of the role of
interest groups, while again occasionally insightful,
misses the mark because Brazilian interest groups are
not by any means without influence. Furthermore, as
this study will show, under certain circumstances,
they are powerful indeed.

The authors of the other two studies, Schneider
on foreign policy making and Hirschman on socioeconomic policy affecting the Brazilian Northeast, concur
in the assessment of a powerful Brazilian executive
which plays a dominant role in the decision making
process.[11] However, each in different ways paints a
considerably more complex picture of that process.
Schnedier, for example, while acknowledging the
clearly elitist basis of foreign policy, alludes to
extensive intramular struggles in the executive
branch.[12] Furthermore, although he does not provide
an explicit analysis of social structure and its impact on the conduct of foreign policy, he does affirm
its importance in influencing the scope and direction
of foreign policy decisions.[13] He relates the conduct of Brazilian foreign policy to the domestic economic and political situation and indicates how
changes in the latter can affect Brazil's conduct in
the international arena. Even nongovernmental groups

whose interest in foreign affairs is sporadic and
whose role is informal and ad hoc at best do occasionally influence foreign policy. Thus, in
Schneider's view, the dominance of the executive and
the weakness of organized interests is not imcompat-
ible with bargaining and the formulation of political strategies. On the contrary, although the immediate policy arena may be restricted, successful
domestic strategies underlie even though they do not
control the conduct of an effective foreign policy.

Hirschman's account of how the Superintendency
of the Northeast (SUDENE) was created likewise affirms the central role of the executive. Nevertheless, this crucial struggle over resources was "marked by bitter and protracted battles, unexpected
switches, and narrow margins of victory rather than
sudden unanimity." [14] In stressing the role of a
wide range of interests in the policy process,
Hirschman situates the powerful executive in a complex and interactive political framework. He observes that presidential interest is a determining
factor in the successful passage of social legislation. However, traditional interests can and do
affect policy outcome, especially during "democratic"
periods when regional political elites can express
themselves through Congress. He concludes that
pragmatism and coalition building are an essential
feature of the Brazilian policy process, and that the
context within which an issue is discussed or implemented substantially affects the definition of the
policy and its application. [15]

The different interpretations of the policy
process, as defined in case study approaches by the
three authors, owes a great deal to the distinct

issue areas they address and the time frame within
which the issues are considered. In contrast to the
other two works, Hirschman's study analyzes a con-
troversial issue whose importance is not only economic, but also social and political. This suggests
that within a reasonably open political situation,
when debate and organizational activity are permitted,
specific traditional interests are more likely to
express themselves on critical social issues which
might affect their political status. Leff himself
notes that the shift of emphasis to basic reforms in
the early 1960s "contrasted with the previous concentration on economic development, without explicit
focus on social and political changes."[16] Unfortunately, he does not examine the implications of
this observation for his own analytical model of the
Brazilian decision making process. When one consi-
ders the relative powerlessness of João Goulart in
his struggle to effect policy changes it becomes
clear that executive power is conditioned by social
and political factors not discussed by Leff. In this
sense, his analysis is incomplete.

In discussing social and foreign policy,
Hirschman and Schneider fill some of the lacunae left
by Leff, but likewise do not present us with a complete view of the political structure and its relationship to decision making in Brazil, in good part
because such was not their intention. They too,
therefore, leave conceptual gaps to be filled out by
additional research and analysis of other issues.
Not all issues, however, are equally useful for exploring the relationship between the policy process
and the maintenance of the political order. Logical-
ly, the greatest yield will come from broad social

issues that affect the definition of authority and
the distribution of power in society.

THE CASE OF LAND REFORM

The controversy over land reform in Brazil during the early 1960s lends itself particularly well to
a study of the relationship between the policy process and the development and preservation of the political system. As one of the most important issues
of the time, land reform was widely debated over a
period of years spanning two different regimes separated by a major political upheaval in 1964. In
fact, the land reform controversy contributed importantly to the overthrow of President João Goulart
and the establishment of the military regime which
has since been in power.

The intensity of discussion and degree of political mobilization generated by land reform make it
an ideal issue for exploring a series of important
questions about the Brazilian authoritarian system.
First, since land reform threatened a redistribution
of property and power, the response of established
elites can be viewed as a measure of the resilience
of political system in coping with social change and
demands for a more equitable distribution of resources. Second, a careful examination of the issue
can help clarify which social groups determine the
nature of the issues that can be raised for overt
policy consideration, under what circumstances, and
with what consequences. Third, this examination
would indicate the terms on which powerful traditional elites accept social and economic change. Finally, this study should tell us something about the

rules, customs, and style of a major political debate
in a traditional authoritarian system.

The discussion of the policy struggle over land
reform begins in chapter two with a review of the
historical importance of the agrarian sector and the
role played by the landed elites in the development
and transformation of the Brazilian patrimonial state.
The historical and institutional analysis is concluded with a close look at the social and political organization of the agrarian sector on the eve of the
land reform debate and a clarification of the apparent as well as the more substantive stakes in the
controversy. Chapter three examines the attempt to
formulate agrarian policy from the perspective of the
executive. Equally important, however, it uses this
major redistributive issue to explore the developmental problems of the Brazilian presidency and to
assess its impact on the political and institutional
crisis which resulted in the fall of the Goulart administration. The next chapter, on the Congress, in
addition to serving the same purpose, provides an
opportunity to examine more closely the influence
and impact of social and economic interest groups in
an openly competitive political situation. It thus
supplies means for evaluating the representativeness,
responsiveness, and efficacy of Brazilian democracy.
This theme is explored in somewhat greater detail in
chapter four, which uses a content analysis of debates in the lower house of the Brazilian Congress to
measure the relevance of party membership, state of
origin, and ideological conviction in the positions
adopted by Brazilian elected politicians in a formal
policy setting. Finally, the last chapter assesses
the nature and impact of the agrarian law and policy

11

implemented by the military government and reviews
the insights provided by this policy analysis into
the nature of the Brazilian authoritarian state, its
strengths and weaknesses, and its methods in coping
with stress and change.

NOTES

1. Barrington Moore,Jr., Social Origins of Dictatorship and
Democracy. Lord and Peasant in the Making of the Modern World
(Boston: Beacon Press, 1966), especially ch.9, "The Peasants
and Revolution," pp. 453-483. See also Samuel P. Huntington,
Political Order in Changing Societies (New Haven: Yale University Press, 1968) especially pp. 291-300, in ch. 5, "Revolution
and the Political Order."

2. See especially Alfred Stepan, editor, Authoritarian Brazil.
Origins, Policies, and Future (New Haven: Yale University
Press, 1973). Philippe Schmitter's essay "The Portugalization
of Brazil?" provides a particularly useful discussion of poli-
tical continuity, and is complemented by Thomas S. Skidmore's
"Politics and Economic Policy Making" in the same volume, es-
pecially pp. 31-43. See also Ronald M. Schneider, Brazil:
Foreign Policy of a Future World Power (Boulder, Colorado:
Westview Press, 1976), pp. 4-5, and Kenneth P. Erickson, The
Brazilian Corporative State and Working Class Politics
(Berkeley: University of California Press, 1977).

3. This argument is fully developed by Raymundo Faoro, Os
Donos do Poder. A Formação do Patronato Político Brasileiro
(Pôrto Alegre: Editôra Globo, 1958).

4. Current interest in this subject owes a great deal to the
path breaking work of Juan J. Linz. Apart from his influential
essay "An Authoritarian Regime: Spain" in Erik Allardt and
Yrjo Littune, editors, Cleavages, Ideologies, and Party Systems
(Helsinki, 1964), Linz's popular lectures at Columbia University gave much food for thought to future generations of scholars. On authoritarianism, generally, see also Samuel Huntington and Clement H. Moore, editors, Authoritarian Politics in
Modern Society (New York: Basic Books, 1970).

5. Juan J. Linz, "The Future of an Authoritarian Situation,"
in Authoritarian Brazil, p. 236.

6. Ibid., pp. 235, 236.

7. Stepan, Authoritarian Brazil, Erickson, The Brazilian

Corporative State, Ronald M. Schneider, The Political System of Brazil: Emergence of a 'Modernizing' Authoritarian Regime, 1964-1970) (New York: Columbia University Press, 1971), Philippe C. Schmitter, Interest Conflict and Political Change in Brazil (Stanford, Cal., Stanford University Press, 1971) are major English language sources on the subject.

8.   Nathaniel Leff, Economic Policy-Making and Development in Brazil, 1947-1964 (New York, Wiley, 1968).

9.   Ibid., pp. 113-118.

10. Ibid., pp. 3-4, 179-181.

11. Schneider, Brazil.   Foreign Policy of a Future World Power; Albert O. Hirschman, Journeys Toward Progress, (New York: Doubleday, 1965), ch. 1 "Brazil's Northeast," pp. 29-129.

12. Foreign Policy, p. 127.

13. Ibid., pp. 165-225.

14. Journeys Toward Progress, p. 57.

15. Ibid., p. 343.

16. Economic Policy Making, p. 168.

13

2. Land, Tradition, and the Socio-Political Order

Since its independence in 1821, Brazil has experienced several major changes of regime, An extended period of stable monarchical rule, the Empire, gave way in 1889 to a highly decentralized,
federated republic ruled by state oligarchies. The
First, or Old Republic was abolished in 1930 by a
revolution which ushered in a fifteen year dictatorship by Getúlio Vargas. From 1945 to 1964, a crisis
ridden Second Republic reintroduced decentralized
and competitive politics within a liberal democratic
framework. Since 1964, Brazil has been ruled by an
overtly authoritarian and politically conservative
military regime.

At first glance, the changes of regime since
1930 in particular invite speculation that they reflect fundamental alterations of the social and economic relationships resulting from rapid modernization. Yet, in fact, Brazil's industrial and economic growth have been achieved not at the expense of,
but within a traditional institutional context. Under the impact of industralization and modernization,
systems of direct, reciprocal social relations and
strong, affective personal ties have not been transformed into impersonal, instrumental relations and
interest oriented class politics. Instead, quasi-

15

familial ties of patronage, clientelism, and mutual
obligation have endured and served as the social
basis of economic transformation.[1] Recurrent political instability, while symptomatic of unresolved contradictions in the political order, should not dis-
tract our attention from the fact that the Brazilian
traditional order has thus far ably survived the
crises of modernization and will probably continue
to do so.

The Brazilian experience of modernization in an
authoritarian framework owes its success to the sustained evolution of a centralized patrimonial state
exercising its authority through a status bureaucracy
while conciliating powerful landholding and urban
economic interests. Traditionally, the legitimacy
of the state's authority has rested on its perform-
ing a guardian role for the society. Less a voice of
the people than an interpreter of their well-being,
the state assumed the role of mediator and impartial
judge, not swayed by partisan interests, and concerned only for the general good of the whole society. At the time of the Empire, this role became explicitly formalized as the poder moderador (moderating power) and officially ascribed to the emperor.
The society he ruled was perceived to consist of non-
competing segments whose special needs and contribu-
tions were to be coordinated into a harmonious whole
in which selfish interests would be constrained by
the benevolent and impartial state.

As economic modernization began to transform
Brazilian society, the patrimonial bureaucratic state
faced the immediate and continuous challenge of successfully altering the traditional basis of its
economy and incorporating new social and economic

16

sectors into the political order in such a way as
neither to threaten its elitist orientation nor erode
its corporatist and statist ethic of legitimacy. To
a considerable extent, its ability to accomplish this
end can be ascribed to the social control exercised
over vast rural areas by a stable and powerful agrarian sector. Once the predominent basis of Brazil's
mercantilist economy, the traditionally organized
agrarian sector preserved its continuity and power
against new economic and political contenders by its
ability to define the limits of acceptable change.
In alliance with military and ecclesiastical power,
the landed elite yielded to necessary modernization
and social change in the urban areas (since it did
not immediately threaten their social control in the
rural area), but rose to overthrow any attempted move
to restructure the traditional patrimonial order.

As Raymundo Faoro indicates, the basic features
of the elitist and status based Brazilian political
order have survived into the modern era.

> This autonomous minority power, neither controlled
> nor limited by the popular will, exercises through
> the bureaucrat, militaryman, and clergyman the
> political patronate that influences and directs
> social movements. . . . Its dominion is assured by
> the fundamental regulation of the economy, /a pre-
> rogative/. . . secured by the patrimonial regime
> and perpetuated in state capitalism. Political
> office holders, even when selected by a majority
> in elections or assemblies, do not succeed in
> surmounting this tutelary shield, but rather,
> accommodate to it, delighting in its privileges
> and attempting to perpetuate themselves /in power/ [2]
> . . . through the enslavement of electoral clienteles.

Periodically, the basic features of this system
have been obscured by an overlay of liberal democracy. The First and Second Republics both seemed to

17

herald a new era of representative, if not precisely democratic government. However, in each case, the authoritarian state reasserted itself after an interval, dispensing with the electoral game and revealing the highly centralized elitist arrangements at its core.

AGRARIAN SOCIETY AND BUREAUCRATIC PATRIMONIAL STATE

Colony and Empire

During the colonial period, from the early sixteenth century until 1808 when King João VI moved the Portuguese court to Brazil in advance of the Napoleonic invasion, the colony's importance to the mother country was based on extractive enterprises, both agricultural and mineral, entrusted to loyal followers. The royal land grant system was based on a 1375 Portuguese law, by which the king parcelled out sesmarias, individual grants of a size that could be cultivated by one individual.[3] Failure to cultivate property could result in the expropriation and redistribution of the land. The purpose of the legislation was both to increase agricultural productivity and to prevent any further accretion in the power of the aristocracy, whose influence the crown was whittling away with the support of urban commerical groups and a newly powerful state bureaucracy.

In the new world, the social and economic impact of the sesmarias was quite the contrary of that intended. The great distance between the colony and mother country, and the enormous expanse of the new territory made efficient administration and central control difficult. More important still was the in-

18

fluence of demographic factors on the pattern of settlement and land use. Portugal's limited ability to send large numbers of settlers meant that except for small and scattered populations of natives, the vast new territory, covering almost half of South America, was largely unpopulated. The existence of a sparse population combined with a great abundance of land did little to encourage the formation of a farmer class. Instead, huge estates controlled by a small planter elite came into being. In the absence of a local labor force, the land was worked by slaves brought from Africa. Brazil thus became a land of great commercial plantations characterized by a highly stratified pyramidal society, in which a large peasant-slave population supported a privileged aristocracy at its apex.

Nevertheless, as Warren Dean observes, from a political standpoint the Brazilian sesmaria system "was entirely functional from the perspective of the Portuguese Crown. The owners of the latifundia /were7. . . in normal times willingly subservient to imperial interests. They sent Lisbon their sugar and hides . . . /and7 remained dependent on Portuguese merchants for credit and slaves." In the scramble for preferential treatment from the mother country, "the Brazilian planters were kept busy plotting against each other rather than the Crown."[4]

In 1821, after the imperial court returned to Portugal, Brazil declared its independence. But, in proclaiming the Empire, it retained the monarchical form of government and continued to be ruled by members of the same royal family. Unlike the Spanish colonies, Brazil did not, therefore, experience a major disruption in its political development at the

19

time of independence. Institutional arrangements and
the relationship of the emperor to his subjects remained largely unaltered. The emperor was vested with
the poder moderador, an arbitral function, based on
an implicit plebiscitary consensus to conciliate conflict and impose unity.[5] In the exercise of his powers, he continued to benefit from intra-elite strife
and governed with the aid of a complex and powerful
bureaucracy. The imperial bureaucracy, a political
legacy of the mother country, enabled the emperor to
avoid exclusive dependence on the landed elite by relying on a functionary, or bureaucratic nobility,
which he could name and remove at will.

The status bureaucracy functioned as an organ of
social control, coopting politically ambitious individuals and socializing them into its comfortable and
prestigious ranks. In this sense, the Brazilian Empire could be compared to other agrarian bureaucratic
empires, of which the Chinese serves as a good example.[6] Eisenstadt observes that rulers of such empires had to find allies "among the groups and strata
whose interests were opposed to those of the more
traditional and aristocratic groups, and who could
benefit from their weakening and from the establishment of a more unified policy." Urban centers, with
their populations of varied economic, cultural, and
professional groups, were particularly useful sources
of such allies, who were recruited not on the basis of
kinship or territorial origin, but of "skill, wealth,
achievement, or political loyalty to the rulers."[7]
By this means, the Brazilian emperor was able to exercise considerable power in the face of traditional
agrarian opposition to the central control of the
state.

Although their direct influence on national policy
was limited, the power of the landed elite was not
negligible. The very vastness of Brazil and the difficulties of communication afforded the landowners
considerable local social hegemony and economic autonomy. But even so, on the local level, the landowners' power was qualified in a number of respects.
Both appointive and electoral systems worked to imperial benefit. For example, until the abolition of
the monarchy in 1889 when many powers were decentralized to the states, the police system was centralized. The imperial government appointed district
police delegates nominated by the imperial chief of
police, who, in turn, was appointed by the emperor.[8]
The electoral system, besides functioning to ratify
appointments made from the top, was skewed to urban
areas, which contained a disproportionate number of
eligible (i.e., literate and propertied) voters.
Thus, the central government skillfully exploited a
variety of control mechanisms at its disposal.

The Old Republic

The establishment of a republic following the
military overthrow of the Empire in 1889 was the first
of two major experiences in the decentralization of
the authoritarian Brazilian state. Since the demise
of the monarchy was linked to the rise of urban republican sentiments that had been responsible for the
abolition of slavery, the change of regime might have
seemed at the outset to be inimical to agrarian interests. Yet, in fact, the contrary was true. The
extreme decentralization of government under the
Old Republic contributed to the preemienence of regional and state interests and of local power. At

this time of the "politics of the governors," national affairs, which included the elections of the president, were settled by a process of adjustment and compromise among state oligarchies. Among these, the most powerful were those of São Paulo and Minas Gerais, which took turns in controlling the presidency in an arrangement called "coffee and milk" for the two states' principal products, coffee and livestock. A network of coroneis, by and large local fazendeiros (landowners), supported the oligarchic political machines and supplied them with votes in return for public power.[9] The coronel, essentially a traditional political boss, controlled a clan which competed with other clans for local control. The coroneis served as links in a chain of reciprocal relations between the municípios (local districts) and state oligarchies, of which the most powerful coroneis were members. The entire rural political system was based on the manipulation of a submissive and dependent rural working population by the large proprietors.

Despite the abolition of slavery in 1888, the social and economic power of landowners did not suffer from the change of regime. The commercial exploitation of agriculture for export purposes continued to be basis of the economy, and rural labor, although freed, remained exploited and dependent. Paid labor had already begun to replace the slave system after a ban on slave trading in 1850. From then until emancipation, the planter class had the opportunity to work out new dependency relations with its labor force.[10] The continued control of large property owners was insured by the chronic exploitation and indebtedness of the laborers and a web of social and political obligations of small owners, sharecroppers,

22

and hired labor to large landowners.

It is from this era of the "politics of the governors" that the stereotype of the all powerful landowner derives. Indeed, during the Old Republic, the power of the planter class to organize the populations dependent on it into efficient political machines was impressive, but it was not unlimited. The countervailing power of the centralized and urban based bureaucracies had been curtailed but not abolished. As Brazil began the process of industrialization, these support sectors of the centralized state together with modernizing elements of the military reasserted themselves forcefully.

The Vargas Dictatorship

The revolution of 1930, which ended the Old Republic, was ushered in by a revolt of young army lieutenants and precipitated by a dispute over the presidential elections of that year.[11] Its importance, however, extended well beyond this specific event. Reflecting the turbulence of the initial phase of modernization, it served as the vehicle for the entry of the middle class into the political arena and set the stage for the political incorporation of urban labor as well.

However, the demise of the Old Republic did not give way, as the middle class had hoped, to a liberal democracy. Instead, the modern industrial era was begun under the auspices of the fifteen year dictatorship of the former governor of Rio Grande do Sul and leader of the insurrection, Getúlio Vargas. In his study of the Vargas regime, Robert Levine notes the irony of the middle class' situation when he observes that

23

the very acts of the government in 1934 and 1935 to
restore democratic procedures through free elections
threatened to return state control to the rural oligarchies, which, through alliances with local bosses,
or coroneis, generally controlled local voting.[12]

In the face of these circumstances, urban middle class
opposition to strongman rule eventually turned to accommodation with what it considered the lesser of two
evils.

Further incentive for collaboration was provided
by what Hélio Jaguaribe has called the "Cartorial
State," a system in which the state exercised a policy of patronage by increasing the number of public
service posts to secure political support in return
for government employment.[13] Lured by the promise of
status and security, the middle class was coopted into implicit collaboration with the corporatist strategy to maintain traditional statist authority, and
"showed itself . . . neither inclined nor able to use
the apparatus of government to bring about a complete
transformation of the country's economic and social
structure."[14] In Jaguaribe's scheme, the expanded
patronage role of the state was an easy alternative to
a more economically rational policy of systematic industrialization. Such a policy might have more effectively resolved the economic needs of the middle
class while contributing toward its independent political development. Yet, in fact, it was this latter
consideration that made "cartorialism" an entirely
rational strategy for a modernizing traditional authoritarian order whose first priority was self preservation. The Vargas years may have been erratic
from the viewpoint of a planned industrial development strategy. But, in retrospect, they must be
judged as a necessary exercise in institution build-

ing to bridge the transition between an agrarian patrimonial past and an industrial future presided over
by a modern authoritarian state.

An important aspect of this effort was the for-
malization of the relationship of society to state
along corporatist lines. The supremacy of the state
as a disinterested arbiter of conflicting interests
and as an expression of the general will of all the
people was reaffirmed. But where little grass roots
associational activity had existed before, Vargas
promoted the establishment of an official syndical interest structure, sponsored and regulated by the
state.[16] By this means, the previously implicit no-
tions of the relationship of concrete socioeconomic
interests to the moderating power of the state were
explicitly defined in a legal framework whose dimensions and rationale, while native in origin, resembled the efforts of European fascist regimes during
that same inter-war period.

According to the dictates of the Consolidated
Labor Code of 1943, the corporatist interest structure was to be organized into syndicates that were to
function as exclusive representatives of their members' interests to the state.[17] The federated interest structure essentially followed the political organization of the nation. Thus, in the industrial
and commerical sectors, where early syndicalization
efforts made greatest headway, separate employer and
employee syndicates were organized for each occupa-
tion at the municĩpio level. Local organizations
were then grouped into state federations which, in
turn, were united into national confederations. By
means of this device, Vargas was able to create an
organized national labor movement where virtually

25

none had existed before. More important still from
the perspective of statist development, that movement
was malleable and dependent, and constituted a political tool in the hands of the government.

From the perspective of the agrarian elite, the
Vargas years constituted the first phase of a long
term process which, while subordinating the rural
power structure to the state, assured its continued
viability and reaffirmed its importance in the political order. In broad lines, the new centralized
structure of the Estado Nôvo resembled that which had
existed under the Empire. The national bureaucracies
regained their strength through central coordination,
and the executive drew its major support from urban
commercial and professional groups, as well as from
the military and the emerging industrial and organized labor groups flourishing under government tute-
lage.

State governments were stripped of the military
and economic prerogatives they had enjoyed under the
Old Republic, but the rural power structure was not
so much humbled as reincorporated by the central government. Vargas shrewdly perceived the utility of
working with rather than against the still powerful
coroneis. In an accommodation with the new regime, the
fazendeiros looked for continued access to federal
power and patronage and noninterference in the rural
social structure. Vargas, in turn, needed at least
the acquiescence of the agricultural elite to pursue
his economic plans, a major aspect of which required
financing industrialization with agricultural, and
particularly coffee profits.[18] In addition, the solid
traditional political control of rural areas could
contribute to general political stability during a

26

turbulent period of rapid urbanization. For these reasons, Vargas willingly refrained from disturbing the traditional social organization of rural areas and the local control of the landed elite. Instead, his agrarian policies emphasized encouragement of modern methods of agricultural production, without making them mandatory. To this end, he created a separate Ministry of Agriculture and a number of federal commodity institutes, and promoted crop diversification and domestic consumption.[19]

But although it was not affected as much as the urban sector, agriculture was not entirely omitted from syndical organization. On October 24, 1945, Vargas signed the enabling regulations for organizing agriculture.[20] Decree law 8127 mandated the establishment of an official representational structure for the rural sector and brought into being the Brazilian Rural Confederation (CRB). Like other confederations, the CRB consisted of local "associations," grouped into state federations. However, in contrast to urban syndical organization, it did not stipulate the creation of separate organizations for employers and employees. In other words, the state effectively refrained from challenging the rural oligarchy's control of its labor force, as well as of renters and small property owners traditionally under its domination. Rural labor expert Arno Schilling has observed that this interpretation of the criteria for membership in the CRB was prompted by a concern on the part of the government that an incipient unionization movement in the countryside might fragment the political control of the latifundium.[21] For the time being, the government preferred to exercise indirect control through its influence with the agricultural elite.

The concentration on urban economic development
and the absence of compelling political and economic
incentives to alter traditional land tenure and productive arrangements temporarily shielded the agricultural sector from the modernizing pressures transforming the urban economy. But the countryside could not
withstand these pressures indefinitely. The inter-
mittent polemics over the agrarian problem during the
post World War II period finally culminated in the
land reform crisis which is the focus of this study.

The Second Republic

Vargas stepped down from power in 1945 in the
face of widespread public demand for an end to arbitrary rule.[22] The new constitution of 1945 formally
established a liberal democracy with a federated republican political system. However, much like the
revolution of 1930, the change of regime produced no
major alteration either in the role of the state, or
the social and economic structure supporting it.

Superficially, the multiparty electoral system
that functioned from 1946 to 1964 and the expansion
of suffrage to all literate persons over eighteen appeared to be a genuine response to the demand for a
democratization of the decision making process.[23] In
fact, it neither rationalized nor democratized that
process. The three major political parties that
emerged in 1945 were firmly rooted in the manipula-
tive and elitist politics of the preceding era. Indeed, two of them, the Social Democratic Party (PSD),
and the Brazilian Labor Party (PTB), were created by
Vargas himself. The PSD, frequently referred to as
the party of the coroneis, consisted largely of the

28

state party machines that dominated the politics of the First Republic. The PTB, referred to as the party of pelegos (government flunkeys)[24] by its detractors, originated in the labor movement organized by Vargas during the Estado Nôvo to serve as his personal machine for controlling labor. Finally, the National Democratic Union (UDN), the party of liberal intellectuals, or bachareis, united an assortment of anti-Vargas groups active in promoting a change of regime. Reflecting their origin, the primary distinction among the parties remained their historical attitude toward Getúlio. The absence of issue orientation in the parties was emphasized by their pragmatic and opportunistic behavior, reflected in high levels of factionalism and coalitions of a purely instrumental nature linking unlikely allies in an inconsistent pattern from state to state and from state to federal level.

Party organization was clientelistic and party loyalties were established principally on the basis of personal ties. Coronelism persisted in the countryside, and in the cities the cabo eleitoral (political boss) or político de clientela (clientele politician) emerged as his urban counterparts.[25] The clientelistic basis of party politics went hand in hand with the Cartorial State, delivering patronage in return for promises of political support.

Not all elections, however, lent themselves equally well to direct, personal, clientelistic manipulation, be it by urban, or even rural political bosses. In particular, clientelistic control tended to be reduced in urban areas where large electorates reflected a higher rate of literacy, which was a requirement for voting. It was also modified to the extent that a specific election was to be decided by

a majority vote as opposed to proportional representation, and in elections whose the geographic scope
encompassed large political units. These conditions
especially prevailed in the elections for president
and state governors.

But a lesser control by political machines did
not by any means turn elections into vehicles of
grass roots interests and issues.[26] On the contrary,
the conduct of majority elections played a companion
role to that of clientelism in blurring issues and
suppressing consciousness of class interests. Since
electoral options in rural areas were already monopolized by rural party bosses, political newcomers
settled on a populist antiestablishment style.[27] Paternalistic in overtones, like clientelism, populism
attracted newly emerging urban constituencies by
appealing to their inarticulate discontent and anomic
frustrations. Populist politicians amassed large
followings not by organizing around distinct issues
or concrete social programs but through charisma and
demagoguery. They fashioned vague promises of nationalist reforms or spiritual rejuvenation which
appealed indiscriminately to a wide social spectrum,
and produced the electoral majorities they needed to
launch and sustain them in power.

Thus, the major political phenomena of Brazilian
electoral politics, clientelism, populism, and coronelismo, were modalities of an authoritarian corporatist system and served as elite strategies in the
ever-expanding competition for power, position, and
status. What changed in the course of electoral expansion and urbanization was not so much the basic
character and purpose of the leadership, but rather,
the strategies used to achieve the leadership's aims

within the existing framework.

The strategy of accommodating demands from the
middle class and urban labor for greater participation by establishing a competitive but still elite
manipulated electoral system ultimately proved to be
a problematic and short term solution. During the
1945-1964 democratic interlude, and particularly
starting with the second (this time elected) Vargas
presidency (1951-1954) Brazil was progressing from
spontaneous industrialization by import substitution
to a phase of planned economic development concen-
trating on establishing a solid domestic industrial
base.[28] The accomplishment of this task would ultimately require modernizing more then just the economy, including the traditional agrarian section. It
also required the revamping of elitist political institutions to reflect the exigencies of popular participation. The most sensitive problem, from this
perspective, was the development of a political framework capable of absorbing newly mobilized social sectors without endangering the security and stability
of the traditional political order which was presid-
ing over the process of economic transformation.

The electoral system did indeed reach out to
erstwhile unpoliticized populations, and in some
sense might have been perceived as an adjunct aggre-
gative mechanism complementing the cartorial bureaucracy. But its nature and functioning aggravated political instability instead of mitigating it. Apart
from sacrificing issue and interest oriented political discussion to vague demagogic populist appeals
and clientelistic manipulation, it introduced and
progressively reinforced a serious contradition between the process by which political leadership was

31

brought to power and the means by which it could exercise that power. Effective decision making still had to be based on the acquiescence of patrimonial and corporatist sources of authority, consisting of conservative, traditional elites. The road to power, on the other hand, increasingly lay in the populist expolitation of an electorate expanding rapidly because of population growth, increasing literacy, and a heightened political consciousness among both urban and rural masses.

These circumstances imposed an especially heavy burden on the nation's political leadership, and particularly the president, in their efforts to produce and effect a coherent developmental strategy. Executive pursuit of developmental goals required striking a balance between their acceptability to traditional elites and international lending institutions, and their nationalist and radically reformist appeal to the masses. The difficulty of this task is underscored by the fact that during the democratic interval, only one president, Juscelino Kubitschek (1956-1961), succeeded in making this formula work. He brilliantly exploited an era of dynamic growth through import substitution measures that projected an image of Brazil as a successful model of democratic modernization for Latin America. It was widely assumed that Brazil had discovered the ideal formula for pursuing populist political strategies and economic development while maintaining the good will and even support of the patrimonial elites. In fact, Juscelino's success lay in exploiting a strategy not of change, but of postponement. In a move reminiscent of Vargas, the problem of the traditional agrarian structure was deferred by a tactical compromise with the landed elite to refrain from altering rural relations. Instead, Juscelino concentrated in his "Target Program" on relatively "safe" economic policy making which promoted urban industrial growth.

However, Juscelino's ability to postpone confrontation with the agrarian issue made his presidency uniquely stable and successful. The political and constitutional crises of the second Vargas presidency, and of the Jânio Quadros and João (Jango) Goulart administrations reflected far more accurately the critical stresses and contradictions between the needs of modernization and the requirements of authority and stability inherent in the traditional Brazilian order. After unsuccessfully grappling with the contradictions of instituting change within a basically conservative and traditional structure allied to a populist mobilizing system, Vargas committed suicide in office in August 1954; UDN-supported Quadros, who came to power with a landslide vote and a promise to sweep the government clean,[29] resigned after seven months in office in August 1961; and finally, in attempting to pass basic structural reforms, including a major land reform, Vargas' protege Goulart was deposed by a military/civilian coup which simultaneously terminated the democratic interlude.

RURAL MOBILIZATION AND LAND REFORM

The Brazilian democratic experiment ended in the midst of a heated debate over land reform that reflected the culmination of a sociopolitical crisis long in the making. Brazil's political leadership had deliberately postponed the problems of integrating the agrarian sector into the modern economy and incorporating the rural lower class into the political process. In so doing, it purchased some time and illusory stability to undergo industrialization. But in the long run, it was impossible to isolate the countryside from the impact of economic and political changes originating in urban areas or from nationalist and exogenous reformist ideologies. Moreover, the economic imperative to integrate the old plantations into a modern framework coincided with increased rural unrest and mounting efforts by leftist urban organizers to politicize and mobilize the camponeses.*

Viewed against the background of the political events of the time, the agrarian issue reflected the convergence and mutual reinforcement of three major issues: 1) the strain between the electoral and authority systems; 2) the threat which social and political mobilization (both urban and rural) posed to the control mechanisms of the patrimonial system; and 3) the dilemma of how to modernize and rationalize an inefficient and exploitative agricultural sector and integrate it into the rest of the economy with a minimum of political disruption.

The Land Reform Issue

By the early 1960s, a sharp increase in rural unrest lent new urgency to a long-standing concern

---

*No single English word fully corresponds to the meaning of camponês. It can mean peasant, countryman, farmer, cottager, all denoting different types of agricultural experience. For this reason, the Portuguese word is used throughout the text, in preference to "peasant."

over the backward state of Brazilian agriculture.
Among traditional landowners and conservative allies
opposition to change in rural areas persisted. But
the political and economic exigencies resulting from
several decades of modernization determined that the
articulation of a coherent agrarian policy could no
longer be postponed. Economic disparities between
the modern industrial sector and the traditional
agrarian sector were becoming increasingly dysfunc-
tional. Additional pressure for change came from
leftist populist politicians who argued for a comprehensive land reform law that would promote social
and economic justice in the countryside.

Ample evidence seemed to support their allegations of the gravity of the rural crisis. The distribution of property and the living and working conditions of rural labor were indicative of systematic
exploitation and an extreme inequality of resources.
According to a 1965 cadastral survey, 50 percent of
all farm land (176,175,062 hectares)* was owned by
1.5 percent of all property owners. The great majority of farm owners, or 63 percent, owned only 6.3
percent of all farm land (11,537,812 hectares), and
44.8 percent of all individually held properties were
10 hectares (24.7 acres) or less. Since twenty hectares was considered the minimum amount of land needed to support a farming family, these figures indicated the existence of a large number of minifundia,
or noneconomic size plots.[30]

This extreme inequality of land ownership cannot
be explained merely by reference to Brazil's large

---

* One hectare equals 2.47 acres.

scale commercial agriculture. Commercial exploitation of land for the production and exportation of
coffee, sugar, cotton, livestock, etc., figured
prominently in the rural economy, and historically
constituted the basis of Brazil's export earnings.
But a full seventy-six percent of all farm properties were officially classified as latifundia, i.e.,
large unproductive or only partially productive
estates. Likewise, the obvious pressure on land indicated by the number of minifundia and latifundia
should not be construed to mean that Brazil had no
reserves of unoccupied land. A considerable investment in extensive infrastructural development could
transform the vast stretches of virgin territory into farm land. However, where the population was most
dense, the quality of land good, and communication
and transportation reasonably developed, the conditions of land ownership were highly unequal and exploitative.

The pattern of land tenure in Brazil and the
role it played in the widespread unrest of the early
1960s was not atypical of Latin America in general.
Nor did it constitute the most extreme case of mal-
distribution. Of seven Latin American countries
studied by the Interamerican Committee for Agricultural Development (CIDA) in the early 1960s, Brazil
had neither the most unequal land distribution, nor
the largest percentage of minifundia or latifundia
(see table 2-1). For example, at that time, the concentration of farm land in the hands of few owners
was far greater in both Chile and Peru, and the problem of minifundia was more accentuated in Guatemala,
Peru, and Ecuador.

But although Brazil's land distribution was not

the worst in Latin America, the rural conditions and tenancy arrangements were deplorable by any standard.[31] In 1963 over half of Brazil's population of 70,967,000, or 39,031,850 people, lived in rural areas.[32] Of the total employable rural population, estimated at about 25,000,000, there were almost five million unemployed rural workers. Furthermore, a vast majority of those fortunate enough to find work did not enjoy a decent standard of living. Fully half of all rural employed persons were salaried workers, sharecroppers, or renters. CIDA's Brazilian report noted that whereas in 1960 the rural populalation constituted 55 percent of the national total, it earned only 28 percent of the national income.[33] Debt peonage and long hours of exploited labor placed the work force at the political and economic mercies of absentee landlords. The physical and social consequences of these conditions were reflected in malnutrition, chronic health problems, high infant mortality, and a rural illiteracy rate of 90 percent, as compared to under 40 percent in urban areas.

Such conditions obviously could not result in maximum efficiency in the use of land or labor, not to speak of converting impoverished farmers into active participants of the consumer economy. Economists were becoming concerned that agriculture might constitute a stumbling block to continued economic expansion. Eventually, "industry is hampered by the low level of effective demand created by low rural incomes at the same time that high prices for agricultural raw materials and for wage goods contribute to high prices for industrial products."[34] To increase food production for internal markets and to expand the domestic market, the traditional rural

Table 2-1

RELATIVE NUMBER AND AREA OF FARM UNITS BY SIZE OF GROUP IN CIDA
STUDY COUNTRIES (PERCENTAGE OF COUNTRY TOTAL IN EACH SIZE CLASS)

	Sub-family	Family	Medium multi-family	Large multi-family
Argentina				
number farm units	43.2	48.7	7.3	0.8
area in farms	3.4	44.7	15.0	36.9
Brazil				
number farm units	22.5	39.1	33.7	4.7
area in farms	0.5	6.0	34.0	59.5
Chile				
number farm units	36.9	40.0	16.2	6.9
area in farms	0.2	7.1	11.4	81.3
Colombia				
number farm units	64.0	30.2	4.5	1.3
area in farms	4.9	22.3	23.3	49.5
Ecuador				
number farm units	89.9	8.0	1.7	0.4
area in farms	16.6	19.0	19.3	45.1
Guatemala				
number farm units	88.4	9.5	2.0	0.1
area in farms	14.3	13.4	31.5	40.8
Peru				
number farm units	88.0	8.5	2.4	1.1
area in farms	7.4	4.5	5.7	82.4

Source: Solon L. Barraclough and Arthur L. Domike, "Agrarian
Structure in Seven Latin American Countries,"
Land Economics 4(1966): 391-424 (© 1966 by the
Board of Regents of the University of Wisconsin
System), 48.

order would have to be transformed through reform and
investment policies.

The argument for a review of agricultural policy
acquired particular urgency under the pressure of
social unrest in the countryside. By the late 1950s,

rural malaise was reflected in land invasions and frequent outbreaks of violence between _fazendeiros_ and _camponeses_, especially in the Northeast and in the states of Minas Gerais and Rio de Janeiro. The concern of conservative elites over the revolution- ary potential of these disturbances was intensified by pressures from outside the country. The recent Cuban revolution and land reform served as fresh re- minders of the revolutionary potential of peasants and workers. In addition, responding to a similar concern, the Alliance for Progress inaugurated by President John F. Kennedy attempted to coax Latin American governments to enact agrarian reforms laws as a condition of receiving aid.[35]

It seemed, then, that for a variety of reasons -- social justice, defensive strategy against potential revolution, international pressure, and continued need for economic development -- a modernizing agrar- ian policy was not merely advisable, but imperative. However, the economic modernization of agricultural posed a major dilemma. Since the social organiza- tion of agriculture constituted the backbone of the Brazilian traditional political order, a modernizing policy implied the modernization of the patrimonial state itself. This required, among other far reach- ing changes, the orderly incorporation of an increas- ingly restive rural work force into the political process under circumstances which the planter class and other conservative elites considered to be espe- cially adverse.[36]

Earlier, the political incorporation of the mid- dle class and urban working class had been accom- plished by the revolution of 1930 and the revival of the authoritarian patrimonial state by Getúlio Vargas.

39

The social and political organization of urban workers by the state prevented the development of the
labor movement into an autonomous political force.[37]
Moreover, during this early phase of industrial
transformation, the cooperation of the traditional
agrarian sector provided an important measure of stability and continuity. Now, agriculture itself was
to be transformed and its social relations reorgan-
ized. Yet, the rural oligarchy's ability to define
in its own favor the terms of lower class incorporation was compromised from 1945 to 1964 by the existence of a competitive, populist democratic system.
The very functioning of that system tended to increase rural mobilization and introduced into the
countryside radical ideologies challenging the hegemony of the landed elite. These circumstances seemed to confirm the fears of landowners and other conservative elites that at the heart of rational economic arguments for agrarian reform lay a direct
threat to the existing political order and the traditional distribution of power and status.

Rural Organization: The Struggle for Control

Brazil had a long history of rural unrest, but
the increase in rural tensions at this time was especially threatening. It occurred in conjunction
with intensive organizational activity in the countryside. Unlike the secondary and tertiary sectors,
the agrarian sector had escaped the full impact of
Vargas' corporatist syndicalization effort during the
Estado Nôvo.[38] Instead of creating separate employers' and employees' organizations, Vargas established a single rural confederation. Rural unionization
remained illegal and rural salaried workers, small

40

owners, renters, and sharecroppers remained under the
unchallenged control of the large planters. Before
the late 1950s only the Brazilian Communist Party
attempted to organize rural labor by establishing a
network of Ligas Camponesas -- not to be confused
with the ligas later associated with Francisco Julião.
Never numerous or strong, the communist Ligas found-
ered after the communist party was again declared
illegal in 1947 following two years of public activity.

Organizational activity among the camponeses re-
emerged in the mid fifties in the most depressed of
Brazil's rural areas, the Northeast. With the assistance of ex-communist party member José dos
Prazeres, the camponeses of the Galiléia sugar plantation organized the Agricultural Society of Planters and Cattle Ranchers of Pernambuco, (SAPP).[39]
SAPP members quickly realized that the survival of
the organization in the face of fazendeiro persecu-
tion would depend on securing political protection.
Prazeres succeeded in getting the support of various
political figures, including that of an ambitious
young lawyer and Brazilian Socialist Party member,
Francisco Julião de Paula. In little time, Julião
became honorary president of what soon grew to be a
network of ligas camponesas, as they were called by
the latifundists "in an attempt to confuse them with
the Liga of Iputinga and other defunct Communist
peasant leagues."[40] The ligas continued to prosper
and extend their network throughout the Northeast.
Their activities received special impetus after reformist Cid Sampaio became governor of Pernambuco in
1959 and sanctioned the forced land distribution
carried out by the ligas earlier.[41]

As talk of agrarian reform became widespread
and the political climate for populist mobilization
became more favorable, other agrarian organizations
began to function. Among the more important were
ULTAB, the Union of Agricultural Laborers and Workers of Brazil, originally created by the communist
party in 1957, and MASTER, the Movement of Landless
Associations, organized by Jango's brother-in-law,
Leonel Brizola, in Rio Grande do Sul. Reformist
Catholic clerics also joined the organizational effort, to the chagrin of their conservative brothers.
Fathers Melo and Crespo sought to counter the influence of the "godless" ligas by setting up church
sponsored unions in Pernambuco and Father Lagé's Radical Catholic Popular Action and Bishop Eugênio Sales'
camponês unions appeared in various parts of the
Northeast.[42] Rio Grande do Sul also boasted a flourishing church organized rural labor movement under
the guidance of Bishop Dom Vicente Scherer. Even the
Ministry of Labor, despite the absence of legislation
legalizing rural unionization, supported camponês
organization in the Northeast.

By the close of 1961 these organizational efforts seemed to be bearing fruit. According to liga
camponesa and ULTAB estimates, their combined membership totalled approximately 550,000 persons.[43] The
ULTAB estimate of 500,000 members may well have been
inflated. But even if it possessed no more than the
200,000 individuals reported by Mary Wilkie,[44] when
added to the ligas' 50,000 and the Catholic church's
45,000 in the Northeast and Rio Grande do Sul,[45] the
rural labor movement demonstrated impressive growth
where virtually no organization at all had existed
as little as five years earlier. The first National

42

Conference of Farm Workers held in Belo Horizonte in
November 1961 assembled 1,400 delegates and over
2,000 other participants who endorsed Julião's call
for a radical land reform.[46]

It was against this background that the Goulart
administration began to press for land reform and
actively and officially supported the rural labor
movement. On March 2, 1963 the president signed into
law the Rural Worker bill introduced two years earlier by Deputy Fernando Ferrari.[47] The law legalized
rural unionization for the first time and mandated
the establishment of separate rural confederations
for agricultural employers and employees. It designa-
nated as rural "employees" all persons who worked for
a rural employer in exchange for money or payment in
kind. A rural "employer" was defined as an individual or corporation, whether property owner or not,
who pursued economic activity in the countryside.[48]

Although the law was clearly a milestone in ex-
tending basic rights to rural workers, its reformist
implications were somewhat ambiguous. By legalizing
rural unions and providing rural workers with a separate confederation, it legitimized and lent special
significance to the unauthorized but widespread rural
mobilization of the last few years. Also, it provided the government with an official role and stake
in the organizational effort. However, because it
uncritically applied urban syndical legislation to
rural areas, the law's reformist potential was suspect. By applying the simple urban legal dichotomy
between workers and employers to the countryside, the
law failed to recognize the diversity and complexity
of agrarian economic relations. Specifically, it
failed to recognize small property and minifundia

owners, renters, and sharecroppers as distinct groups
with unique problems and interests. Commenting on
their perception of agrarian problems, Adolpho
Puggina observed:

> The owner of a small property, sharecropper, and
> renter, are as interested in agrarian reform as
> are salaried rural workers, and if organized into
> their own unions would constitute a powerful force
> that could not only make demands, but also, and
> principally, offer invaluable collaboration with
> the authorities in the execution of an agrarian
> reform.[49]

Since these groups were not legally recognized as
"employees" they automatically fell into the legal
category of "employers" and therefore under the control of the large landowners.

In this context, the complacency with which
large landowners initially regarded the introduction
of the bill in Congress is understandable.[50] Apart
from their expecting minimal enforcement of the law,
they perceived that it allowed them to retain control over a considerable part of the rural occupational population. As the breakdown of the Brazilian rural occupational structure in table 2-2 indicates, salaried workers constituted 33.3 percent of
economically active individuals in rural areas.
Since medium to large landowners, that is, those capable of hiring workers, constituted 11 percent of
the economically active rural population, the large
landowners retained effective control of the remaining 55.6 percent, or 9,007,200 people and their dependent families. But João Goulart soon demonstrated
that an apparently innocuous law could become a
threatening instrument in the hands of even a weak
president determined to generate new sources of political support.[51] The complacency of the landowners

Table 2-2

RURAL OCCUPATIONAL STRUCTURE, 1965

Category	Number	Percent
Owners with employees............	1,783,832	11.0
Owners without employees.........	7,441,868	45.9
Renters..........................	220,000	1.4
Sharecroppers....................	1,358,000	8.4
Salaried workers.................	5,396,300	33.3
Total.....................	16,200,000	100.0

Source: Estrutura Agrária Brasileira, and Chacel, p.114.

was effectively shaken when they found that the government intended to use the law as the basis of an
official rural mobilization effort. Moreover, to
force their compliance and participation in this unionization campaign, Goulart withheld the official
federal subsidy from the landowners' confederation.
The CRB consequently found itself in the anomalous
position of promoting syndical reorganization to its
member associations to maintain its financial solven-
cy while simultaneously repudiating the regime responsible for the distasteful policy.[52]

The resulting rapid increase in the number of
rural organizations did not, however, imply grass
roots autonomy for the camponeses. It was soon apparent that political protection from landowner oppression was to be purchased only at the cost of political dependence on urban leftist leaders and submission to their manipulation.[53] The campaign for

45

improved rural conditions through syndicalization became another springboard for politicans working their
way up the political system. Everyone, including the
government, wished to establish control over what
seemed certain to become a major new constituency
and source of populist political support. The stakes
were much enhanced by the active support of many
leftist politicians, including the president, for
suffrage reform giving illiterates the right to vote.
Such a move would have dramatically increased the
size of the rural electorate. But it promised little
political independence to the potential camponês voters.

Resisting submission to the demands of official
clientelistic cooperation was obviously unrewarding.
The ligas, perhaps the most independent of the rural
groups, were harassed rather seriously even as early
as the parliamentary period when they adopted an
anti-administration position on the plebiscite.
Julião publicly opposed a return to the presidential
system in 1963 and urged liga members to abstain from
voting.[53] Shortly thereafter, Julião was thrown out
of the Brazilian Socialist Party and later denied
membership in the PTB.[54] Having fallen out of favor
with the official leftist forces in power, the ligas
were not invited to enjoy the benefits of its patronage. On November 23, 1963 the new labor minister
Amaury Silva, called a meeting of ULTAB, Popular
Action, and the PTB. In compliance with the provisions of the Rural Worker Law they were instructed to
form the national Confederation of Agricultural Workers, CONTAG. Pointedly excluding the ligas, the new
organization "brought together 263 legally recognized rural syndicates, 480 rural syndicates in the pro-

46

cess of receiving legal status, and twenty-nine
Federations of Rural Syndicates from nineteen of the
Brazilian states."[55]

But if the ligas camponesas experienced autonomy only briefly, other groups enjoyed none at all.
ULTAB from the very first was manipulated by the
communist party as a complement to its urban policy.
When CONTAG formed, the official federal endorsement
stifled most of the independent tendencies of the
member syndicates. The fate that had befallen urban
labor afflicted the new camponês unions as well. Indeed, in bringing the camponeses under official control, the populist urban leadership, especially that
of the PTB and minor leftist parties, used urban
labor unions as an ally.[56] In the Brazilian political
context modernization of rural relations clearly
implied a new form of clientelistic exploitation by
the political leadership. In the early 1960s, a number of political actors openly competed for control
of rural labor. Among them were landowners, the left
populist government of João Goulart, two factions of
the Catholic church, and several individual political
leaders. It is doubtful that the camponeses themselves ever figured as serious contenders for the
control of their own destiny.

Landowner Interest Organization and Class Solidarity

The landowner leadership, aware for some time
that modernization would eventually affect the traditional agrarian sector, was concerned that the process of transition not undermine the political authority and economic preeminence of the fazendeiros
in the countryside.[58] They favored an agrarian policy
that would provide traditional planters and latifund-

ists the time and means to adapt their properties to
modern capitalist commercial exploitation. This concern motivated early participation of the CRB in discussions of agrarian policy initiated by Jânio
Quadros in 1961.[59] The official landowner position
advocated the replacement of old forms of agrarian
production with a new capitalist agriculture confirm-
ing the inviolability of private property. For the
fazendeiros "land reform" signified not a redistribution of property, but the initiation of the poor
into the ways of private enterprise. In their view,
this was best accomplished not by special government
distribution programs for landless camponeses or
minifundia owners, but by camponês recourse to commercial loans for the purchase of land.[60] CRB president Iris Meinberg condemned expropriation as a
waste of resources and an incentive to speculation
and rural unrest.[61] He felt the capitalist transformation of agriculture should be undertaken with
the aid of an extensive government program which
would benefit the entire agrarian sector and not just
the poor by providing agricultural credit, training
and extension programs, tax incentives, price supports, agroindustrial development incentives, and
colonization of virgin lands.[62] Finally, conceding
that land was not always used efficiently by owners,
the CRB guidelines admitted the possibility of taxing unproductive property.[63]

There were some indications, however, that this
official CRB platform was presented by the leadership as a gruding attempt to accommodate to some inevitable change without alienating its traditional
constituency. Edgar Teixeira Leite, spokesperson
for the rural confederation for many years and prob-

ably its single most influential publicist, proposed
to the National Economic Council in July 1961 that
the term "agrarian reform" be stripped of its negative redistributive connotations and rendered more
acceptable to conservative landowners.[64] However, his
suggestion that agrarian reform be redefined as "everything that aims at benefitting agriculture" seemed less an argument for land reform than an admission
that many landowners were not ready for the CRB's
progressive capitalist proposals. In fact, while
planters already involved in commercial export farming found these plans unexceptional, traditional
latifundists thought them threatening to the old pa-
triarchal order.

With Goulart's succession to the presidency and
the accentuation of the land reform controversy, the
landowners confederation found itself in a particularly unhappy situation. Jango's land reform plans
and rural mobilization drive placed the confederation in the uncomfortable position of depending fi-
nancially and politically on an executive apparently
bent on destroying the power and coherence of the
landed sector. Charges by some planters, such as the
wealthy coffee growers of the Brazilian Rural Society
(SRB) that the official confederation leadership consisted of government errand boys appeared to have
some merit.[65] The SRB complained that the official
agrarian leadership, no less _peleguista_ or subservient than that of labor, subsisted on the contribu-
tions of large planters while servily supporting government policies inimical to grower interests.[66]

However, the confederation could do little to
alter its legally established relationship to the
government. In theory, the general membership of the

49

confederation elected the leaders representing the
agricultural sector to the government. In fact, a
candidate's political acceptability to the government served as the single most important criterion
for his selection as an official. The undisguised
political dependence of the confederation on the
government caused it to be perceived by landowners
generally as an unreliable defender of planter interests against official policies. Consequently, the
active membership of the rural confederation tended
to be small, as indicated by table 2-3. At a time
when the employable rural population approximated
twenty-five million people, associational membership
consisted of approximately one-tenth of one percent
of the total.

Table 2-3

MEMBERSHIP, BRAZILIAN RURAL CONFEDERATION

Year	Number of Associations	Number of Members
1946	108	18,453
1950	213	32,284
1955	1,130	179,558
1960	1,802	240,129
1961	1,867	229,034
1966	2,087	317,866

Source: Agricultura Brasileira, p.6.

The rural confederation's unenviable position
between a threatening government and a contemptuous
constituency underscored the special problems the
CRB's official status generated for the leadership

when it attempted to influence the conduct of government policy. Only official confederations were legally recognized as representatives of their sector's interests. But the official interest structure served more as a conduit for government views to the organized sectors than it did for the expression of the membership's opinions and needs. In a system which heavily stressed executive prerogatives in patronage and decision making, a president hostile to planter interests, as was João Goulart, effectively closed off that sector's access to the single most important official source of policy making. Before the 1963 plebiscite on parliamentarism, when he clearly needed conservative support for advancing the date of the referendum, Jango had made an effort to ingratiate himself with the landowners. In his single formal meeting with representatives of the "patronal" class in 1962, he assured them of his respect for private property and moderation. Following the restoration of the presidential system, he appeared to have reconsidered his need for the planters' support. As Goulart's reliance on radical mass politics increased, so did the distance between him and the landowners. The president saw no further utility in meetings or exchanges.[68]

The planters, in fact, seemed able to do little to neutralize the land reform threat while working within a framework which automatically gave the executive an upper hand. Even in the face of a serious challenge to their security, landowner interests demonstrated limited capacity to organize effectively for influencing a specific policy under legislative consideration. They were rather ineffectual as an interest group, as is demonstrated by later discussion in this study of the Congress and the policy process. Their power to influence policy, however inimical to their interests, was undercut by the state regulated interest structure and the susceptibility of clientelistic politics to central manipulation and patronage. Yet, paradoxically, as a major pillar of the traditional political order, the planter class could muster considerable power in defense of that order. It was curiously like an army regiment armed with no small or intermediate weapons and carrying only major destructive artillery. Although increasingly ineffective when defending its particular interests in battle, it nevertheless played a decisive role in winning the war in which it shared a stake with other conservative elites. The planter class did, in fact, literally arm itself in the defense of the patrimonial state and found ready allies in the defense of the political order.[69]

The willingness of other groups to join the fazendeiros in the defense of private property was based on their perception of a common political threat and not on any special sympathy for landowners or their problems. Concern over the agricultural bottleneck in the developmental scheme may have been widespread among economists and planners, but it enjoyed little currency in Brazilian business circles. Business representatives generally admitted having little knowledge of agriculture and perceiving no particular relationship between the performance of their particular sector and agriculture. The consequently felt little motivation for becoming involved in the technicalities of agrarian discussions.[70]

When in rare instances individual business leaders did demonstrate an interest in rural problems,

they generally showed little concern for the poverty
and exploitative in which the rural masses lived.
Antônio Delfim Neto, a _paulista_ economist destined to
become minister of finance under presidents Costa e
Silva and Garrastazú Médici following the 1964 revolution, typified knowledgeable business opinion at the
time. Observing that the agricultural crisis was
blown entirely out of proportion, he pointed out that
the agrarian growth rate was 4.2 percent in 1963 --
an entirely acceptable figure, in his view, considering that the population was expanding at a rate of
2.8 percent. He categorically opposed any land redistribution program and maintained that agrarian
problems could be alleviated by means of education,
health, and industrialization programs.[71]

Only in one instance did the agrarian problem
receive thoughtful attention from business leaders.
The newly formed IPES (Institute for Social Research
and Study) brought together business and military
leadership to review systematically Brazil's national
developmental problems.[72] A handsome volume on land
reform figured as one of its most outstanding achievements.[73] This volume's significance extended well beyond the fact that a military industrial brain trust
had produced a major review of the agrarian problem
and proposed solutions. Rather, it lay in the fact
that soon thereafter IPES members became officials of
the 1964 military government and the agrarian study
became the basis of an agrarian reform law enacted by
the military regime in 1964.

But in the early sixties, such specific interest in the complexity of agricultural economics and
social relations was rare.[74] The intense concern of
conservative elites over the possible consequences of

land reform was motivated primarily by political considerations. Thomas Pompeu Accioli Borges, Brazilian
representative of the United Nations Food and Agricultural Organization, observed that despite passing
reference to the desirability of a land reform to expand the internal market, the employer's group
staunchly opposed an agrarian reform law. Whatever
its potential benefits, they perceived it as a means
to limit individual control over private property.[75]
Speaking for the Federation of Commercial Associations of Brazil, Afrânio de Carvalho condemned the
Goulart proposal for undermining democracy and making
"a tabula rasa of the constitutional principles of
property and free enterprise." The government should
consequently adopt a substitute policy "in which
implementation of the reform would be more on the
basis of individual initiative than of state action."[76]
The organization's president, Paulo de Almeida Barbosa
expressed his concern more bluntly, saying that the
Goulart proposal for a redistribution of property
would lead to communism.[77]

This opinion was fully shared by the conservative wing of the Catholic church, which dissociated
itself from the views of reformists such as Dom
Helder Câmara, the bishop of Recife, and other clerics
advocating social and economic reform. In a well
publicized book attacking land reform (Agrarian Reform, a Matter of Conscience), three bishops and two
lay persons movingly, if inaccurately, depicted the
landowner as a hardworking man who acquired his property by the sweat of his brow. Arguing from a clas-
sically corporatist position, they appealed for the
preservation of traditional social and economic
distinctions since national well being depended on the

"intimate cooperation /resulting from/ prudent and
harmonious /sectoral/ differentiation. It is on this
that social peace is founded."[78] Lest their argument
be perceived as no more than a moral appeal, in a
subsequent publication they suggested that anyone
participating in a land reform program could be ex-
communicated.[79]

Within the armed forces, as within the church,
the range of opinion on land reform varied considerably. The military as an institution was not single-
mindedly opposed to a reform program. Indeed, Jango
found support for his reformist goals among prominent
figures within the top brass, such as General Segadas
Viana, Admiral Angelo Nolasco, Brigadier General
Clovis Travassos, General Machado Lopes, and General
Pery Bevilacqua. In a more conservative, developmen-
talist vein, some military officials played an important role in IPES and contributing to its studies.
But the weight of military opinion did not seem to
be on the president's side. A study of the land reform issued by the alumni of the National War College
favored an evolutionary agrarian policy and condemned
drastic redistributive measures.[80] This attitude seemed closely related to the evidence of rising social
unrest.[81] Overall, military concern with land reform
mirrored a primary preoccupation with the ultimate
political consequences of a policy which would challenge the established order, contribute to a lessen-
ing of political control over the masses and lead to
a radical syndicalist regime.

This concern, shared equally by landowners and
other employer groups, provided the basis for conspi-
ratorial activity by the "producing classes" against
the Goulart administration. Jango's program did not

just threaten the standing of one sector of the economy in relationship to the others (as for instance, was the case earlier when agriculture bore the financial burden for industrialization). By attacking private property and encouraging lower class unrest, his land reform program imperilled the security and position of all the elites. Always uneasy about Goulart's succession to the presidency, conservative opposition began to plot the demise of his administration under the cover of the Superior Council of Producing Classes (CONCLAP), the peak employers' confederation. CONCLAP held monthly meetings in the year preceding Goulart's fall, and played an important role in cooperating with the church and other groups in mobilizing public opinion and organizing anti-government demonstrations.[82]

As Jango eventually abandoned any effort to deal with the conservative constraints on presidential authority, he began to take unilateral action to initiate reforms which the Congress had previously balked at passing. The armed forces watched the rising tide of social disorder and mass unrest with growing apprehension. Hard line opponents of Jango had long been plotting an overthrow among themselves. They now gained adherents from among the constitutionalists who had favored an orderly succession following Quadros' resignation in 1961. Concern over the crisis of the state was clearly superseding preoccupation with constitutionalism. Goulart sealed his own fate when he supported military unionization and interferred directly with the authority of commanding officers. This coalesced his military and civilian opposition and precipitated a coup against him.

Given the furor Goulart's proposal for land reform caused in conservative circles and the role it
played in his overthrow, it may seem initially para-
doxical that one of the first acts of the new military regime of General Humberto Castelo Branco was
the passage of an agrarian reform law. Like
Goulart's proposal, it aimed to transform the traditional rural economy. But Castelo's land law differed from that of his predecessor's radical redistributive proposal in its emphasis on modernization within
an explicitly capitalist mode. Ultimately, the major
issue raised by the agrarian controversy was not
whether the traditional, socially exploitative and
economically backward rural arrangements could be
preserved. Rather, it was whether in making the
transition to the modern era the landed class would
preserve its status and prerogatives. The accomoda-
tionist process of development pursued by the corporatist capitalist state required the planters to share
power with other, industrial and technological elites
at the top of the socioeconomic pyramid. But it
maintained the statist authority and elitist strati-
fication system of the traditional political and social orders. The alternative solution represented by
João Goulart was ultimately no less statist. But
state power would be exercised by a militant vanguard
in the name of, although not necessarily for, the
masses, who would supplant the traditional elites as
the new sociopolitical status group.

NOTES

1. See especially Anthony Leeds' insightful essay, "Brazilian
Careers and Social Structure: An Evolutionary Model and Case
Study," American Anthropologist, 66, Part I (1964), 1321-47.

2. Raymundo Faoro, Os Donos do Poder. A Formação do Patronato Político Brasileiro (Pôrto Alegre: Editôra Globo, 1958), pp. 44-45.

3. Faoro, p. 15, and Caio Prado Júnior, The Colonial Background of Modern Brazil (Berkeley: University of California Press, 1967), pp. 134-138.

4. Warren Dean, "The Problem of Latifundia in Nineteenth Century Brazil," Hispanic American Historical Review, (November 1971), p. 607.

5. Two particularly excellent discussions of this subject are Faoro and João Camilo de Oliveira Torres, A Democracia Coroada (Rio de Janeiro: Livraria José Olympio, 1957).

6. For an extensive treatment of this subject, see S.M. Eisenstadt, The Political Systems of Empires (New York: The Free Press, 1969). See also Barrington Moore, Jr., The Social Origins of Dictatorship and Democracy. Lord and Peasant in the Making of the Modern World (Boston: Beacon Press, 1966), chapter 4, "The Decay of Imperial China and the Origins of the Communist Variant."

7. Eisenstadt, pp. 14, 15, and 21.

8. João Camilo de Oliveira Torres, Estratificação Social no Brasil (São Paulo: Difusão Europeia do Livro, 1965), p.45. See also Juarez Rubens Brandão Lopez,, A Crise do Brasil Arcaico (São Paulo: Difusão Europeia do Livro, 1967).

9. For a discussion of coronelismo, Victor Nunes Leal's Coronelismo, Enxada e Voto (Rio de Janeiro: Livraria Forense, 1949) continues to be the best work on the subject, although more recent works are available. See, for instance, Marcos Vinicios Vilaça and Roberto Cavalcanti de Albuquerque, Coronel, Coroneis (Rio de Janeiro: Edições Tempo Brasileiro, 1965). For a fine study of Rio Grande do Sul during the republican era see Joseph L. Love, Rio Grande do Sul and Brazilian Regionalism, 1882-1930 (Stanford, Cal.: Stanford University Press, 1971).

10. See Stanley Stein, Vassouras, A Brazilian Coffee County, 1850-1900 (Cambridge, Mass: Harvard University Press, 1957), and Gilberto Freyre, Ordem e Progresso (Rio de Janeiro: Editôra José Olympio, 1959). Alberto Passos Guimarães, Quatro Séculos de Latifundio (Rio de Janeiro: Paz e Terra, 1968) deals specifically with these dependency relations in chapter 4.

11. For an in depth discussion of the Vargas regime, and especially of the beginning of the Estado Nôvo, see Robert M.

Levine, The Vargas Regime: The Critical Years, 1934-1938 (New
York: Columbia University Press, 1970). See also John W. F.
Dulles, Vargas of Brazil: A Political Biography (Austin: The
University of Texas Press, 1967).

12. Levine, pp. 14-15.

13. Helio Jaguaribe, Economic and Political Development. A
Theoretical Approach and a Brazilian Case Study (Cambridge,
Mass.: Harvard University Press, 1968), p. 144. See also his
"A Crise Brasileira," Cadernos de Nosso Tempo, No. 1 (October-
December 1953).

14. Economic and Political Development, p. 143.

15. Ibid., p. 144.

16. Philippe C. Schmitter's Interest Conflict and Political
Change in Brazil (Berkeley: The University of California
Press, 1971) provides the most comprehensive study of interest
organization in Brazil.

17. The code, as Schmitter explains, "upheld voluntary membership, sindicalismo único (limiting recognition to one sindicato
for each profession), representation of professional categories
. . ., separate but equal treatment and parallel organization of
workers and employers, and a series of government controls coordinating the activities of the associations and subordinating
them to rational interests." It also introduced "a system of
membership categories, a syndical tax, a comprehensive system of
labor courts, and a minimum wage law." Ibid., p. 115.

18. John Wirth's The Politics of Brazilian Development, 1930-
1954 (Stanford, Cal.: The Stanford University Press, 1970) provides an overview of Vargas' social and economic policies. For
a case study of the transition from agriculture to industry,
see Warren Dean, The Industrialization of São Paulo 1880-1945
(Austin: The University of Texas Press, 1969). Broader discussions of Brazilian economic and industrial development are
provided by Werner Baer, Industrialization and Economic Development in Brazil (Homewood, Ill.: Irwin, 1965), and Celso
Furtado, The Economic Growth of Brazil (Berkeley: The University of California Press, 1963).

19. Levine, p.13.

20. These were based on Decree Law 7038 of November 10, 1944,
and made explicit in Decree Law 8127 of October 24, 1945, which
stated that every município was to have a rural association in
which all who "practiced rural activities by profession" were

qualified for membership.

21. Arno Schilling, "Sindicalização Rural" (Mimeo, Pôrto Alegre, 1969), p. 17.

22. A general discussion of Brazilian Politics from 1930 to 1964 can be found in Thomas E. Skidmore, Politics in Brazil, 1930-1964 (New York: Oxford University Press, 1967).

23. For a discussion of Brazilian political parties during this period see Phyllis Jane Peterson, "Brazilian Political Parties: Formation, Organization, and Leadership, 1945-1959" (unpublished Ph.D. dissertation, University of Michigan, 1962), and Marta Cehelsky, "The Brazilian Political Party System, 1945-1964. A Comparison With the Post-Independence Party System of India" (typescript, 1967).

24. Literally, a pelego is a sheepskin placed under a saddle. But, as the Pequeno Dicionario Brasileiro da Lingua Portuguesa explains, colloquially, it is a term used for "the Ministry of Labor's more or less covert agents in labor unions." Tenth edition, compiled by Aurelio Buarque de Hollanda Ferreira with José Baptista da Luz (Rio de Janeiro: Editôra Civilização Brasileira, 1963), p. 912.

25. Paulo Singer, "A Politica das Classes Dominantes," in Octavio Ianni, et al., Política e Revolução Social no Brasil (Rio de Janeiro: Civilização Brasileira, 1964), p. 74. See also Francisco Weffort, Politica de Massas," in the same volume and his "Raizes Sociais do Populismo em São Paulo," Revista Civilização Brasileira I (No. 2, 1965), and Juarez R.B. Lopez, Desenvolvimento e Mudança Social (São Paulo: Companhia Editôra Nacional, 1968), and Leeds, "Brazilian Careers and Social Structure."

26. Glaucio Ary Dillon Soares in "The Sociology of Uneven Development," in Irving Louis Horowitz, editor, Revolution in Brazil (New York: Dutton),1964 argues that urbanization and industrialization, which are associated with the weakening of traditional ties, correlate positively with the rise of disciplined "ideological parties" and a relatively lower ratio of opportunistic party alliances. Juarez Lopez suggests ("Desenvolvimento," p. 229, n.4) somewhat more realistically that it is more probable that the type of political organization and style referred to by Soares is not the result of new economic and ideological interests, but merely an instrumental response on the part of politicians attempting to attract a new type of electoral support.

27. The one major work on populism in English is Ghita Ionescu and Ernest Gellner, editors, Populism, its Meanings

and National Characteristics (London: Weidenfeld and Nicolson, 1969). The chapter on Latin America by Alistair Hennessy does little, however, to enhance our understanding of Brazilian populism. More useful is Torcuato di Tella's "Populism in Latin America" in Claudio Veliz, editor, Obstacles to Change in Latin America (New York: Oxford University Press, 1965).

28. See particularly Jaguaribe's analysis of these developments in Economic and Political Development, especially chapter 10, "The Process of Development," and chapter 12, "The New Structural Crisis."

29. Quadros received 5,636,623 votes, or 48.29 percent of the 11,679,679 valid votes cast. Institute for the Comparative Study of Political Systems, Brazil Election Factbook Number 2. September 1965 (Washington, D.C.: ICOPS, 1965), p. 56.

30. Instituto Brasileiro de Reforma Agraria (IBRA), Estrutura Agrária Brasileira (Rio de Janeiro: IBRA, 1967).

31. The body of literature on agricultural conditions in Brazil, and especially the Northeast, is enormous. The Bibliografia sobre Reforma Agrária published by the Instituto de Ciencias Sociais (Rio de Janeiro: Universidade do Brasil, 1962) listed 1,164 publications on the subject. Among the best sources are: Passos Guimarães, Quatro Séculos de Latifundio, Manuel Correia de Andrade, A Terra e o Homem no Nordeste (São Paulo: Editôra Brasiliense, 1963), Euclides da Cunha, Rebellion in the Backlands (Chicago: University of Chicago Press, 1944), Antônio Callado, Os Industriais da Seca e os "Galileus de Pernambuco," (Rio de Janeiro: Civilização Brasileira, 1960), and Manuel Diegues Júnior, População e Açucar no Nordeste do Brasil (Rio de Janeiro: Comissão Nacional de Alimentação, 1965).

32. Instituto Brasileiro de Geografia e Estatistica, Anuario Estatístico do Brasil (Rio de Janeiro: 1954-1976).

33. CIDA, Land Tenure Conditions and Socio-Economic Development in Brazil (Washington, D.C.: Pan American Union, 1963), p. 24.

34. Armin K. Ludwig and Harry W. Taylor, Brazil's New Agrarian Reform. An Evaluation of its Property Classification and Tax Systems (New York: Praeger, 1969), p.3. See also essays by Julian Chacel and Gordon Smith in Howard Ellis, ed., The Economy of Brazil (Berkley: The University of California Press, 1970), and Henrique de Barros, A Estrutura Agrária como Obstáculo a Ação Agronômica. A Reforma Agrária como Problema Econômico (São Paulo: Escola de Sociologia e Política de São Paulo, 1954). Warren Dean notes this type of concern as early

61

as the 1920s and 1930s. Industrialization of São Paulo, pp. 130-133.

35. Between 1960 and 1963 alone, eight nations complied by passing agrarian reform laws. They were: Chile, Colombia, Costa Rica, Dominican Republic, Guatemala, Nicaragua, Panama, and Venezuela.

36. As Samuel Huntington has observed, "The ability of the political system to survive and of its government to remain stable depends upon its capacity to counter /the/ revolutionary appeal /of urban groups/ and to bring the peasants into politics on the side of the system." Political Order in Changing Societies (New Haven: Yale University Press, 1968), p. 292.

37. The best discussion of labor in Brazil is to be found in Kenneth P. Erickson, The Brazilian Corporative State and Working Class Politics (Berkeley: University of California Press, 1977).

38. See Arno Schilling, passim, Schmitter, chapter 8, and Edgar Teixeira Leite, "Aspectos da Sindicalização Rural no Brasil," Jurídica No. 31 (abril-junho 1966).

39. Clodomir Moraes, "Peasant Leagues in Brazil," In Rodolfo Stavenhagen, editor, Agrarian Problems and Peasant Movements in Latin America (New York: Doubleday, 1970), pp. 462-464. See also Cynthia N. Hewitt, "Brazil: The Peasant Movement of Pernambuco, 1961-1964," in Henry A. Landsberger, editor, Latin American Peasant Movements (Ithaca, N.Y.: Cornell University Press, 1969), pp.324-398, and Mary E. Wilkie, "A Report on the Rural Syndicates of Pernambuco" (Mimeo, Rio de Janeiro, Centro de Pesquisas em Ciências Sociais, 1964).

40. Ibid., p. 465.

41. Ibid., pp. 477-78. Ironically, the sympathy of the state government had negative consequences for the ligas according to Moraes. "Once given title to their land by the state, the Galileia peasants lost interest in the politics of the agrarian struggle." The Galiléia liga, which until this time had been the center of the organizational effort, dwindled to a few dozen quarelling members by 1961.

42. Ibid., p. 491.

43. Ibid., p. 482.

44. Wilkie, p. 7.

45. Gleba, Vol. 8, No. 85 (1962), p. 37.

46. Moraes., pp. 497-498.

47. Originally a PTB deputy from the state of Rio de Janeiro, Ferrari ran as one of Jânio Quadros' two vice presidential candidates, and lost. Disillusioned with the politics within the PTB and by the PTB's conduct in the national political arena, he formed his own party, the Labor Renovation Movement (MTR). His death in an airplane crash in 1963 cut short a promising political career.

48. Estatuto do Trabalhador Rural, Title I, Art. 1, and 2. Adriano Campanhole, editor, Legislação Agrária (São Paulo: Editôra Atlas, 1969.)

49. Adolpho Puggina, Reforma Agrária. A Reforma das Reformas (Pôrto Alegre: FETAG, 1968) p. 16.

50. Confederação Rural Brasileira, "Relatório das Atividades da Confederação Rural Brasileira em 1965" (mimeo, Rio de Janeiro, 1965), pp. 1, 2. See also, Teixeira Leite, "Aspectos da Sindicalização," p.4, and his "Aspectos do Complexo Agrário Brasileiro," Carta Mensal (Orgão do Conselho Técnico da Confederação Nacional da Industria, Vol. 15, No. 180 (1970), p. 13.

51. Goulart's support for the bill initially was quite lukewarm. It was not until after its passage that he appeared to realize fully its political potential. Correio da Manhã, March 6, 1963, p. 6. Cited hereafter as CM.

52. For a discussion of the CRB and the syndicalization issue see Teixeira Leite, "Aspectos da Sindicalização," and Confederacao Rural Brasileira, "Sindicalização Rural," (mimeo, Rio de Janeiro, n.d.).

53. The political potential of the campanonês organization has been the subject of considerable controversy. Anthony Leeds argues that the relationship between Julião and the ligas was basically clientelistic and paternalistic and that Julião was a typical elitist Brazilian politician in a new ideological disguise. "Brazil and the Myth of Francisco Julião," in Joseph Maier and Richard W. Weatherhead, editors, The Politics of Change in Latin America (New York: Praeger, 1964). Benno Galjert takes a similar position in a debate with Gerrit Huizer in América Latina. Huizer, in contrast, sees the organizational activity among the camponeses as the beginning of class consciousness and independent political action. Benno Galjert, "Class and 'Following' in Rural Brazil, "América Latina, Vol. 7, No. 3 (julho-septembre 1964); Gerrit Huizer, "Some Notes on Community Development and Social Research," América Latina, Vol. 8, No. 3 (julho-septembre 1965).

54. Francisco Julião, editor, Ligas Camponesas: Outubro 1962 -- Abril 1964 (Cuernavaca: CIDOC, 1969). The following message was typical of his campaign: "Under the presidential regime, 70% of the land was in the hands of 2% of the latifundists. Under the parliamentary regime, nothing has changed. Therefore, there is no difference /between the two/. There is another option. A vote for agrarian reform is not to vote in the plebiscite." Ligas, p. 63.

55. Jornal do Brasil, January 3, 1963, p. 1, and January 6, 1963, p. 3. Cited hereafter as J B

56. See, for example, the Correio da Manha, June 4, 1963, p. 16, for a review of the General Confederation of Labor's plans for strikes and bus caravans, and July 11, 1963, p. 4 for an account of the CGT's organization of the week of Basic Reforms.

57. Moraes, p. 492.

58. Teixeira Leite, "Aspectos do Complexo Agrário," p. 7.

59. Officially, the CRB deplored what it referred to as the chronic official neglect of agriculture. (See in particular, CRB, "A Agricultura Brasileira, Diretrizes para um Plano de Ação." Memorial da CRB as Exmo. Senhor Presidente da Republica, Doutor Jânio da Silva Quadros. Gleba, Marco 1961, p. 8; and Ben Hur Raposo, A Reforma Agrária para o Brasil (Rio de Janeiro: Fondo de Cultura, 1965), pp. 24, 25). In so doing, it conveniently ignored the possibility that latifundio owners might have found this neglect particularly advantageous in the short term.

60. Teixeira Leite, "Reforma Agrária Brasileira. Destinação Econômica e Social da Terra," Observações sobre o Ante-Projeto da Comissão Especial (mimeo, Rio de Janeiro, Conselho Nacional de Economia, n.d.), p. 16.

61. CRB, "A Agricultura Brasileira," pp. 25, 26.

62. Ibid., pp. 11, 39, 40, and passim. See also Gleba, Vol. 7, nos. 74-77 (1961), p. 11, and J B , July 28, 1961, p. 8.

63. "A Agricultura Brasileira," pp.25-26.

64. "Reforma Agrária, Destinação, p.4.

65. In interviews I conducted in São Paulo, SRB representatives did little to hide their contempt for the official leadership.

66. The notion that the leadership of the official employers' group is subservient to and manipulated by the state has gained greater currency with the study of Brazilian corporatism. Faoro was an early advocate of this view. More recently, Schmitter and Erickson have taken this position.

67. During interviews I conducted, confederation leaders stressed that it was pointless to elect someone of whom the government did not approve. Schmitter makes a similar observation, indicating that official supervision discourages grass roots participation.

68. C M , June 22, 1963, p. 15.

69. J.B., July 29, 1961, p. 3. The rumor reported by the Jornal do Brasil was substantiated in interviews I conducted with landowners, particularly in Rio Grande do Sul and Minas Gerais.

70. The reaction of a high official of the National Confederation of Industries to my request for an interview on agrarian policy was somewhat more extreme than most but not atypical. He felt sure at first that while looking for the National Confederation of Agriculture, as the CRB was retitled in 1966, I had erroneously wandered into the wrong confederation offices.

71. Antônio Delfim Neto, "Agricultura e Desenvolvimento," Mundo Econômico, No. 10 (1967), p. 5. See also the Estado de São Paulo, October 20, 1963 for a declaration of the Technical Council of Social and Political Economy, signed by Delfim and other prominent economists, industrialists, and businessmen.

72. Two branches of IPES were established in 1962, one in São Paulo, the other in Rio de Janeiro. The carioca branch functioned as a research group and survived the 1964 crisis. The paulista group, which functioned more as a political pressure group and organizing center for anti-Goulart demonstrations and other activities ceased to function after the 1964 military take-over. A review of IPES membership lists and executive committee meeting minutes read like a "who's who" in Brazilian government. IPES files, typescript and manuscript, 1962-1966, passim.

73. Instituto de Pesquisas e Estudos Sociais, A Reforma Agrária: Problemas, Bases, e Soluções (Rio de Janeiro: IPES, 1964).

74. Robert Kaufman, Chile's Agrarian Reform (Washington, D.C.: ICOPS, 19 p. 36).

75. Thomas Pompeu de Accioli Borges, "Novos Rumos para a Reforma Agrária Brasileira" (typescript, Rio de Janeiro, 1968, internal document of the Grupo de Trabalho Sobre Reforma Agrária), p.6.

76. C M , May 5,1963, Caderno 2, p. 20.

77. Paulo de Almeida Barbosa, quoted in A Gazeta (São Paulo), May 8, 1963. Also, see A Folha de São Paulo, May 16, 1963 for similar statements by the Federation of Industries of São Paulo.

78. Dom Orlando Rodriguez, Dom Antônio de Castro Maier, Dom Geraldo Proença Sigaud, Plínio Correa de Oliveira and Luiz Mendonça Freitas, Reforma Agrária, Questão de Consciencia (São Paulo: Editôra Vera Cruz, 1960), p. 20.

79. Dom Orlando Rodriguez, et al., Declaração do Morro Alto. Programa de Política Agrária Conforme os Princípios de Reforma Agrária, Questão de Consciencia (São Paulo: Editôra Vera Cruz, 1964), p. 10.

80. Accioli, "Novos Rumos," p. 5.

81. J B , February 4, 1962, p. 3. Also see Visão, May 31, 1963, p. 11 for a statement on the subject by General Kruel.

82. Schmitter, p. 197. Also see pp. 195 for the origins of CONCLAP.

3. Presidential Politics and Land Reform

Although they differed sharply in style, personality, and the general tenor of their administration, João Goulart and Humberto Castelo Branco coincided in their perception of land reform as one of the principal issues of the time. In confronting land reform, they grappled with a political and economic problem that could no longer be postponed. Their respective programs, while implying distinct consequences for the political system, both recognized that the old Brazilian agricultural order was doomed.

Despite their apparent ideological differences, Goulart and Castelo also concurred on a number of the major measures they considered necessary for the resolution of the land reform problem. Specifically, both insisted that the land statute be accompanied by a constitutional amendment which would make it possible to pay for expropriated land in bonds. Both considered expropriation a necessary feature of any land reform program. Neither reduced the agrarian problem to simple economic terms, but emphasized instead its profound social dimension. Finally, both presidents favored an agrarian policy consisting of a combination of land redistribution, colonization, and agricultural support measures. The two presidents diverged principally in their perceptions of the true purpose of land reform. For Castelo it was the modernization of agriculture in a capitalist framework; for Jango, it was the restructuring of the social order.

AGRARIAN PROPOSALS

Despite the furor it caused, Goulart's land reform proposal was not exceptionally innovative. Nearly two hundred agrarian bills were introduced in the Congress in the course of Brazilian history. In the sixties alone, the reports, conference resolutions, vague commitments, and proposals were transformed into twelve major bills and laws, some radical, other revisionist.[1] These twelve major proposals are listed in table 3-1, indicating sponsorship of the measure, its purpose, and the action taken on it. Except for their divergence on the issues of the means and justification for the expropriation of property, the proposals are similar in many respects. The definition of priorities and objectives usually included a statement about social justice and the need to create a class of independent middle class farmers. Frequently, there would follow a list of measures aimed at stimulating agricultural production. Among these, progressive taxation was a favored strategy. By contrast, Brizola's and Goulart's idea of forced leasing found support only among the radical left politicians. All the proposals suggested some form of land expropriation and redistribution and extensive programs of colonization, agricultural extension, credit, and technical assistance.

The basic similarity of the bills and proposals is not surprising. First of all, they reflected the temper, orientation, and knowledge of the times and of their sponsors. In the second place, they were cumulative. Earlier bills served as a basis for the elaboration of new ones. Finally, all bills written after 1961 were strongly influenced by the work of the Milton Campos commission. Named informally for its coordinator, Senator Milton Campos, the Special Commission for Agrarian Reform was established by President Quadros in May 1961.[2] Its purpose was to study the agricultural situation in Brazil and to build on the work begun by the National Commission for Agricultural Policy established by Getúlio Vargas in 1951. The Campos commission was charged with recommending legislative and executive measures necessary to alter the land tenure system, promote rural justice, and increase agricultural productivity.[3] The commission's findings, advocating a combination of land reform and agricultural assistance, influenced all subsequent legislation. Specifically, all ensuing proposals supported the following measures: 1) the creation of a productive farming class out of the impoverished and often landless camponeses and rural workers; 2) the alteration of land use patterns to bring unused land under cultivation; 3) colonization of available unused land; and 4) the improvement of agricultural productivity through credit, technical assistance, and extension programs. The Campos commission also recommended the creation of a Superintendency for Agrarian Reform.

Despite these similarities, the areas of disagreement among the agrarian proposals of the 1960s were not minor either in terms of their importance or in the degree of controversy they generated. Controversy focused on a constitutional amendment permit-

Table 3-1

MAJOR AGRARIAN LEGISLATION, 1960-1970

Sponsor	Proposal	Purpose	Action Taken
Dep. Fernando Ferrari, PTB/MTR Rio de Janeiro May, 1961	Rural Worker Law	Protection of rights of rural workers, right to unionize, regulation of contracts, work conditions, social security	Enacted into law as law No.4214, March 2, 1963
Dep. José Joffily, PSD, Paraíba, July, 1961	Agrarian Reform Bill	Moderate redistribution within confines of constitution; extension, colonization programs	None
Dep. Gileno de Carli, PSD, São Paulo, July, 1961	Agrarian Reform Bill	Emphasis on colonization, productivity, credit	None
Sen. Milton Campos, UDN, Minas Gerais, August, 1962	Agrarian Reform Bill	Creation of farmer class; similar to Joffily proposal, better elaborated	Passed by Senate Dec. 1962, defeated by Chamber, Aug.1963

Sponsor	Measure	Description	Outcome
Dep. Leonel Brizola, PTB, Rio Grande do Sul, March, 1963	Agrarian Reform Bill	Radical alteration of tenure system based on expropriation with alteration of constitution	None
Pres. João Goulart, March, 1963	Agrarian Reform Bill	Radical land redistribution based on constitutional amendment	Action depended on amendment, below
Pres. João Goulart, April, 1963	Constitutional Amendment	Make possible expropriation of land payable in bonds, maximum indexation ten per cent	Rejected October, 1963
Dep. Aniz Badra, PDC, São Paulo, August, 1963	Agrarian Reform Bill	Create middle-class farmers; closely resembled Campos bill	Passed only by Chamber, April, 1964
Pres. João Goulart, March 13, 1964	Expropriation Decree	Expropriate property bordering roads, railroads, dams, within ten kilometers	Signed by President March 13, 1964, based on Decree Law 3365, June 21, 1941
Pres. Castelo Branco, May, 1964	Constitutional Amendment	Make possible expropriation of land payable by fully indexed bonds	Passed as Amendment No. 10 to Constitution Nov. 6, 1964

71

Table 3-1 - Continued

Sponsor	Proposal	Purpose	Action Taken
Pres. Castelo Branco, May, 1964	Land Statute Proposal	Increase productivity, promote social justice in countryside, distribute land, colonization; heavy reliance on progressive taxation	Passed as Land Statute, Law No. 4504, Nov. 30, 1964
Pres. Costa e Silva, April, 1969	Institutional Act Number 9	Facilitate expropriation procedure, making it administrative, not court matter, regulate compliance with taxation	Signed by president, April, 1969
Pres. Emílio Garrastazú Médici, July, 1970, February, 1971	Decree Law No. 1110; Decree Law No. 68153	Abolish land reform and agrarian development institutes created in 1964. Substitute National Institute for Colonization and Agrarian Reform (INCRA) with an emphasis on colonization	Signed by president, July, 1970, February, 1971
Pres. Emílio Garrastazú Médici, July, 1971	Decree Law No. 1179	Create Program of Redistribution of Land and Stimulus to the Agro-Industry of the Northeast (PROTERRA); alters tax incentives system tied to land program. Focus: creation of agro-industry	Signed by president, July, 1971

Sources: Based on record of congressional debates, newspaper accounts, J. Motta Maia, Iniciação a Reforma Agrária (Rio de Janeiro: Mabri, 1969), and Adriano Campanhôle and Hilton Lôbo Campanhôle, Legislacao Agrária (São Paulo: Atlas, S.A., 1974, 6th edition).

72

ting land expropriation to be compensated in the form of long-term bonds rather than in cash. This would materially alter the relevant provisions of the extant 1946 constitution which made land expropriation both difficult and unfeasible because of its cost. Article 141, paragraph 16 stated:

> The right of property is guaranteed, except in cases of expropriation for reasons of public need, or utility, or for social benefit, by means of previous and just compensation in money. In the case of imminent danger, such as war, or internal disorder, the competent authorities may use private property, if the public good so requires, with the right to subsequent indeminization remaining assured.[4]

Although article 147 of the constitution provided that the use of property was subject to public welfare and that the state had the power to redistribute property, such expropriation was possible only on the basis of full payment in cash prior to the act of expropriation itself.

Under these rules, the funds required for a widespread expropriation program would have to be enormous and an agrarian reform bound by these restrictions would have a very limited application. By specifying the type and time of payment, the 1946 constitution precluded the use of long-term bonds, which would neither be negotiable as currency nor redeemable until a specified number of years had passed. Understandably, anyone advocating a comprehensive land reform within the existing framework would insist on a revision of the constitution. A constitutional amendment aimed at modifying the provisions on expropriation to permit a more rational, long range repayment program constituted the core issue of the debate on land reform and the bone of contention between the president and Congress.

The Legislative Process

To facilitate comprehension of the two presidents' relationships to Congress while trying to secure both a land reform law and an amendment to the constitution, it will be helpful to review briefly the constitutional framework of the Brazilian legislative process during the post World War II period.

According to the Brazilian constitution of 1946, bills could be introduced by the president and by any member or commission of either of the two houses of Congress, the Chamber of Deputies and the Senate. Within each house, twelve permanent committees exist to rule on specific matters, such as constitutional problems, finance, education, etc. The respective membership of these committees, which report on specific aspects of legislation under consideration, ranges from a handful in either house, to close to a hundred in the budget and commerce committee of the Chamber.[5] Until 1964, there was little difference in the type of bill that could be introduced by either house. Since the revolution, however, monetary bills can be introduced only by the president or the Chamber of Deputies. A bill proposed by the executive, both before and after the revolution, has had to be considered first by the Chamber, and if approved, passed on to the Senate. To become law, an ordinary bill must be passed by a majority vote in both houses, and signed by the president. A two-thirds vote of both houses is necessary to overrule a presidential veto.

The first decrees issued by the revolutionary government in 1964 altered the legislative process.

74

Article four of the first Institutional Act provided
the following:

> The President of the Republic may send the National
> Congress bills on any subject, which must be acted
> on within thirty days . . . from day of receipt in
> the Chamber of Deputies and in equal time in the
> Federal Senate: . . . /if no action is taken/ they
> will be considered /automatically/ approved.

Furthermore:

> If he considers the matter urgent, the President of
> the Republic can call on the National Congress to
> consider the bill in a joint session in thirty
> days. . . .

If Congress failed to act within the time limit, the
bill automatically became law.

Equally important, if not more so, were the
changes introduced in the procedure for amending the
constitution. Before April 1964, proposals for amendments could be introduced only by a fourth or more of
the Chamber or of the Senate, or by over half of all
state assemblies acting within two years' time.[6]
After the revolution, the president himself could propose amendments. When the executive acted on this
possibility and sent a proposed constitutional amendment to Congress, the national legislature was required to act on it within thirty days of its receipt.
The amendment was approved if the proposal received
an absolute majority of votes in both houses of Congress in two sessions held not more than ten days
apart.

These differences in rules had a decisive impact
on the manner in which Congress considered presidential bills before and after 1964. While Goulart was
forced to resort to various means of applying political pressure to hasten the legislative process,

Castelo had considerably greater institutional leverage. Most of the latter's bills, although they could
be amended and altered by Congress, automatically became law unless specifically rejected within thirty
days. In the area of constitutional amendments,
Castelo also had an advantage in that he himself
could propose one, without the concomitant need to
rely on his political party to secure the signatures
of a fourth of the members of both houses. The
thirty day time limit was also a clear incentive for
Congress to take action of some kind. With these
changes, the position of the executive in relation to
Congress was strengthened. This did not mean, however, that the president could afford to ignore the
legislature. Congress could defeat bills as well as
approve them, and had not yet been reduced to a rubber stamp, as it would be in 1968.

JOÃO GOULART AND LAND REFORM

Jango's handling of the agrarian reform controversy was intimately related to his political standing. He fortuitously became president following
Jânio's unexpected resignation and in the face of
considerable political opposition. It was based on
fears that Vargas' protege, who admired both Lenin
and Argentine ex-president, Juan Perón, would favor
the creation of a radical syndicalist regime.
Goulart succeeded to office principally because the
military was divided on whether to allow him to take
power, and because there were strong currents of both
military and civilian opinion supporting the preservation of constitutional legality. However, although
the opposition could not prevent Goulart from taking

power, it exacted a paralyzing compromise. Goulart took office, not as head of the presidential system established since 1946, but as the president of a new parliamentary regime designed to circumscribe the power of the chief executive.

While it lasted, the parliamentary framework indeed constrained the new president in the exercise of his powers. Jango's eventual success in having it abolished did not, however, prove an automatic means to effective executive authority. The more serious obstacles were not to be disposed of so easily. Most important among these difficulties was an institutional crisis rooted in the contradiction between the oligarchic distribution of political power and the populist requirements of the electoral system since 1946. The conditions of effective rule remained elitist and oriented toward informal negotiation among the economically and socially powerful members of the corporate elite. The presidential road to power, on the other hand, was based on populist mass appeal to an expanding electorate. As a consequence, the Brazilian president was elected to office by one constituency, which enabled him to "reign;" but he could "rule" effectively only with the support of another. To the extent that the policy process had to be conducted within this schizophrenic framework, discussion of fundamental issues dealing with the nature of the system tended to an impasse. The populist promises on one hand, and the corporatist elitism on the other, implied two mutually exclusive alternatives in the social definition of problem solving. Jânio Quadros' earlier attempts to eliminate this contradiction and to provide a common base for both election of officials and for their governing, ended in frustration and his resignation after seven months in office.

A second difficulty centered on the personality and political beliefs of João Goulart. Within a difficult institutional situation, Jango was regarded with utmost suspicion and distrust by established political forces, both in the anti-Vargas National Democratic Union (UDN) party and even in the Vargas-founded Social Democratic Party (PSD). Goulart's single important power base was in the labor unions and in the Brazilian Labor Party (PTB). In the eyes of the Brazilian political establishment, Jango's political career, labor affiliations, and apparently keen interest in the ideology and strategies of former Argentine president, Juan Perón, rendered him untrustworthy. Furthermore, he was perceived as a political opportunist who could not even be trusted to maintain any idological position with integrity. For conservatives and moderates alike, the only thing worse than a dogmatic ideological leftist, was an unprincipled, unpredictable, and opportunistic leftist. Since effective executive rule was premised on at least a tacit acceptance by these political and military elites, their disapproval meant that he was most unlikely to succeed where Jânio had recently failed.

A third difficulty, as Ronald Schneider points out, consisted in Goulart's having been "manufactured by Vargas as an instant national figure," and in lacking the experience normally gained by national politicians who had been governors and/or national legislators. "His hop-skip-and-jump career -- straight from the ranch to the cabinet, then on to the vice presidency, and accidental accession to power -- was all too apparent in his relations with the military."[7]

-- And, we might add, with most groups and institutions outside of labor.

Finally, these structural and situational difficulties were compounded by Goulart's self image
and his perceptions of his own role as president.
Goulart did not want to be known historically as the
man who was constantly defeated by political circumstances. He wished to make an historical impact and
to be remembered for some major contribution:[8]

> Often viewed as a weak personality for a major
> political leader, he was not prone to run risks
> for abstruse principles or causes in which he had
> no great stake. A shrewd political manipulator
> with no great vision and prone to look for the
> path of least resistance, Goulart was not, how-
> ever, lacking ambitions that transcended the mere
> holding of office. . . . He did not wish to go
> down in history as a weak and indecisive man, un-
> able to deal effectively with the problems of
> Brazil. He was not disposed either to become a
> powerless tool of the established commercial,
> industrial, and agricultural groups or to be up-
> staged. . . by a more authentic and popular figure
> on the left. . . . His irresoluteness stemmed from
> a lack of training in dealing with technical prob-
> lems and a lack of patience in studying complex
> matters.[9]

As Schneider's assessment of the president's personality indicates, Goulart would have had trouble mas-
tering the art of governing even in the best of circumstances. Yet he came to power under the worst
possible conditions. As reflected in his handling of
the agrarian reform bill, in his struggle with Congress, and his relationship with other groups he
would not be able to rise above historical constraints
or his personal limitations.

Goulart's brief presidential career can be divided into four distinct periods. The first period,
that of the parliamentary regime, began with his in-

augration on September 7, 1961 and ended with the
return of the presidential system following the plebiscite of January 6, 1963. The second period, notable for his collaboration with the "positive left,"
lasted from January to June 1963. Then, from his June
cabinet reshuffle to December of the same year constituted the third period, an interval with emphasis on
radicalization, but without overstepping the limits
of the opposition's political tolerance. The final
period, from December 1963 to his ouster in March,
was characterized by the abandonment of the established political process and a unilateral attempt to exploit radical mobilization strategies.

Parliamentary Interlude: September 1961 - January 1963

The fourteen months of the parliamentary regime
were the calm before the storm. Although it had looked
like the only solution possible at the time, parliamentarism was not, as it turned out, a very happy one.
It may not have been directly responsible for increasing inflation, declining investment, flight of
capital, slow down in economic activity, and increased social unrest. But the new system appeared to be
incapable of confronting these problems. Goulart's
claim that he could not possibly influence the situation or improve it while his hands were tied seemed
plausible enough.

The parliamentary arrangement aggravated Goulart's
difficulties with Congress. The president's own
Brazilian Labor Party, the PTB, was a minority party,
contending with an obviously hostile National Democratic Union, and a suspicious Social Democratic
Party. The PSD might have been convinced to cooperate, but only in exchange for some direct benefit to

itself. The conservative opposition, which included many pessedistas (PSD members), formed the Democratic Parliamentary Action coalition (ADP), to shore up the parliamentary regime as a means of circumscribing Goulart's influence. The president faced a challenge from the left as well in the form of an alliance between the followers of Deputy Fernando Ferrari of the state of Rio de Janeiro, and the compactos, or left wing of the PTB, which denounced Goulart's brand of politics for its lack of ideological consistency.[10] Ferrari, in fact, seemed to be challenging Goulart's leadership of the left and pushing for the formation of a new party, which would be a fusion of Ferrari's Labor Renovation Movement, the National Labor Party, and factions of the Christian Democratic and Brazilian Labor Parties.[11] Perhaps on a more embarrassing personal level to Goulart was the challenge to his leadership by his own brother-in-law, Leonel Brizola, governor of Rio Grande do Sul at the time. To make matters worse, it could not even be said with any degree of assurance that Goulart was actually in control of the National Liberation Front (FLN), organized as a leftist answer to the ADP. The efficacy of the FLN as a policy instrument was in any case questionable. While in theory representing a reformist position on behalf of the people, the FLN's effectiveness was impugned by its seeming irrelevance to the needs of the increasingly radicalized masses and its inability to deliver promised reforms.[12]

Two immediate political tasks dominated the agenda in the second half of 1962. One was the congressional interim election in October 1962. The second was the preparation of the plebiscite. Goulart concentrated on the plebiscite, paying relatively little

81

attention to the bitterly contested election in which
structural reforms were the main issue. The plebiscite had been originally scheduled for 1965 and
Goulart intended to move it up by a full two years.
His strategy was two-pronged. First, he deliberately
undertook to allay the fears and suspicions of traditional and conservative sectors of opinion. While
making pointed reference to growing social unrest and
strikes, Goulart's piously conservative speeches emphasized the need for carefully prepared and rational
reforms and for austerity measures to deal with the
financial crisis. Second, he relied on the negative
impression parliamentarism itself was creating. For
Goulart the series of governmental crises and cabinet
reforms served the purpose of demonstrating that the
parliamentary system was unweidly, inefficient, and
incapable of solving the pressing problems of the day.
If not attended to, Goulart stressed, the impasse
might result in revolution. Enough politicians and
military figures were swayed by this argument and by
the political and social unrest to have the plebiscite
moved up to January 6, 1963.

Besides pressing for a return of the presidential
system, which was perhaps, as Schneider says, Goulart's
·   ·le greatest accomplishment, the president was pre-
ɟaring another major project -- a program of "Basic
Reforms." Far more interesting than the boring details of the financial crisis, "the idea of such reforms," Skidmore points out, "appeared to offer Jango
the opportunity of making an historical reputation for
himself and also a way of building his own political
following."[13] The keystone of this program, which he
launched on May Day in 1962, was land reform.

In emphasizing land reform, Goulart was taking advantage of an issue that had already achieved considerable public prominence. Internationally, continued aid from the Alliance for Progress was linked to enactment of a land reform law. This foreign pressure underscored a series of domestic events. The work of the Milton Campos commission urgently calling for an agrarian policy coincided with predictions of a poor harvest in 1962. Food shortages were already being experienced. Concern with the state of social unrest and the drop in agricultural productivity motivated several states to confront the issue on their own. Governor Carvalho Pinto of São Paulo, who at a later point would become Goulart's minister of finance, succeeded in having the paulista legislature pass an Agricultural Revision Law in November 1961. The mildly reformist statute emphasized rural credit, technical assistance, and some colonization. A more radical redistributive bill would have stood little chance of passage in the face of opposition from the state's powerful commercial export sector.

Modest as it was, however, the new paulista law generated some excitement and alarm. Not a few paulistas perceived it as a dangerous encroachment on constitutional rights. Defenders of the rural status quo in other parts of the country viewed it as the first crack in the dyke of their social, economic, and political hegemony. Indeed, in a general sense, their assessment had some merit since there seemed to be a move afoot in various states to enact some sort of agricultural policy.[14] Brizola's agrarian reform activities, which included rural unionization and some land expropriation by the Gaucho Institute of Land Reform were perceived as especially threatening.

Since the major resource available to state legislatures and governors for inducing reforms was the power of taxation, the rural opposition mobilized a campaign against this potentially dangerous prerogative.

The ruralists' strategy was astute. They would
have been most unwise to launch an anti-land reform
campaign in an era when being against reforms was
equivalent to being against motherhood.[15] Instead,
the opposition operated from behind a more popular
facade -- that of "municipalism." In essence a movement for decentralization of authority and financial
powers, particularly the powers of taxation affecting
rural property, municipalism argued for the devolu-
tion of these powers to local governing units. The
ruralists reactivated the old campaign, and formed an
alliance with the municipalists, who alone had never
been able to achieve their aim. Congressional passage
of Constitutional Amendment No. 5 on November 21,
1961, transferring the power of rural property taxation from states to municípios made any discussion of
agrarian reform through state initiative academic.
After the 230 to 4 vote in favor of the Senate-spon-
sored amendment was tallied in the Chamber of Deputies, one federal deputy, in a moment of candor,
gloated over the "end of agrarian reform."[16] Clearly,
if there were to be any land reform at all, it would
have to come from the federal government.

As if in recognition of this fact, and also in
preparation for what promised to be a stiff political
battle, the annual governors' conference meeting in
Araxá in early June of 1962 placed the discussion of
agrarian reform high on its agenda. In spite of considerable opposition to a pronouncement of any kind,
the conference in an official statement endorsed

agrarian reform based, however, on the provisions of
the constitution.[17] The radical and reformist governors, who opposed the official position taken by the
conference, contended that any agrarian reform not
based on constitutional amendment would not be worthy
of its name. They banded together to form a separate
organization, which immediately produced the Declaration of Goiânia, a strong statement in favor of
sweeping structural reforms.[18]

The lines of battle formed around the issue of
constitutional reform. Goulart, in the meantime,
maintained a low profile. His first priority was the
plebiscite, and until he achieved his aim, his behavior remained very circumspect and politically dis-
creet. His speaking engagements included an appearance at the fourth Ruralist Conference on January 25,
1962, at which he assured the landowner membership of
the Brazilian Rural Conferation that the purpose of
a land reform could never be that of taking productive land away from owners and distributing it indis-
criminantly to those who do not produce. "If anyone
has the great social duty to give away land," the
president reassured the fazendeiros, "that someone is
the State."[19] Jango conceded that the constitutional
provisions on expropriation might make land redistribution somewhat more difficult, but he was willing to
accept that limitation. He informed his audience that
he considered himself to be more conservative on the
point of expropriation than even the Milton Campos
commission, which was not renowned for its radical
tendencies.

Goulart's low profile on agrarian matters carried over to his relations with the Congress as well.
The Milton Campos commission finished its period of

study and research, and submitted its moderate recommendations to the president. Campos himself introduced into the Senate an agrarian reform bill based
on the work of his commission. Goulart had Prime
Minister Tancredo Neves routinely present Congress
with a request for a number of agrarian legislative
measures. They included a bill on land rental, a
bill to create an executive organization for agrarian
reform, an amendment to return the land tax to federal jurisdiction, and one to alter the conditions
for expropriation based on social need. In addition,
the president endorsed the Rural Worker Law which
had been introduced by Fernando Ferrari in 1961.

Oddly out of context, before the legislature
adjourned, it passed a law establishing a Superinden-
dency for Agrarian Reform, SUPRA, which was to replace the shorlived National Council on Agrarian Reform founded in February. The new agency regrouped
already existing departments and possessed no additional independent financial or administrative resources. Its jurisdiction was unclear and there was
no indication of how its parts were to be coordinated. Originally, SUPRA's creation had been recommended
by the Special Commission on Agrarian Reform as an
integral part of a comprehensive land reform program.
The absence of such a program at this time and the
nature of the new agency strengthened the impression
that the measure was passed on the eve of the plebiscite primarily for political motives.

Responsible Government and the "Positive Left," January-June, 1963

The second phase of the Goulart administration
began with the plebiscite of January 6, 1963, in
which seven million votes were cast in favor of a

return to the presidential system. Goulart, who had become president through succession, interpreted the vote as a personal mandate. He had the formal powers and hence the opportunity to demonstrate the seriousness of the commitments and promises he made throughout 1962. His attempt to live up to these commitments resulted in his experiment with the "positive left," a sector of center-left political opinion committed to fundamental change but based on realistic economics and moderation. San Tiago Dantas, whom the Congress had vetoed a year earlier as prime minister, became minister of finance and leader of the new cabinet which also included Celso Furtado as minister of planning and Almino Afonso, minister of labor, representing the radical left.

The new year started off on a seemingly serious, and responsible footing with the unveiling of the Three Year Plan of Economic and Social Development drawn up by Celso Furtado. Economic stablization and fiscal responsibility were important objectives, but they would not be achieved at the expense of fundamental reforms. The plan included provisions for tax, administrative, banking, and agrarian reforms.

The measures which Furtado advocated for agrarian development were moderately reformist, and tied integrally to the rest of his development plan. The specific measures included: 1) expansion of production relative to demand; 2) correction of distortions and deficiencies in the export crop sector; 3) increased productivity and improvement of the quality of primary products destined for the internal market; and 4) a position on land expropriation: "All lands considered necessary for the production of food, and which are not being used, or are being used for other

87

purposes with yields inferior to the standards re-
gionally established, could be expropriated according
to our Plan, with long term payments."[20]

The land reform proposal actually forwarded by
the president to Congress in March went well beyond
the Furtado plan. It called for a constitutional a-
mendment making it possible to pay for land expropriated by bonds, and proposed a program of forced
leasing of unused lands. It also outlined a policy
of technical and financial supports to agriculture
(extension programs, credit facilities, colonization,
and technical assistance) to complement the land
distribution program.

Two aspects of this agrarian proposal make it
seem that although he was still working on his alliance with the positive left, Jango was also getting
ready to abandon it in favor of the "negative" left."
First, as a part of the overall policy of conciliation and bridge building, the president formally entrusted his reform program to the PSD. This move
appeared conciliatory but incongruous. The PSD was
based primarily on rural political machines, represented some of the most traditional landed interests,
and seemed an unlikely sponsor of reformist legislation. The Correio da Manhã speculated that perhaps
Goulart did not really want reforms: "Amaral Peixoto,
Benedito Valadares, Abelardo Jurema, and others. These
men /known for their conservative politics and land
based power/ 'accepted' the stewardship of the reforms. Let's wait and see."[21] Goulart underscored
his conciliatory stand by declaring at a cabinet meeting that he had no wish to interfere in the congressional debate on agrarian reform, since the national
legislature should be able to deliberate freely,

without pressure from the executive. In addition, he stressed that he did not wish in any manner "to strengthen the cause of those who wish the most radical reform."[22]

These overtures to the moderates were somewhat belied, however, by a second feature of the agrarian reform proposal. The draft of the constitutional amendment sent to the Chamber of Deputies stipulated that the maximum allowable correction for inflation on the land reform bonds would be ten percent. This meant that at a time when the rate of inflation had reached an all time high of eighty percent per year, the actual reimbursement would be a fraction of the stated value of the land at the time of expropriation. In addition, the amendment draft provided that the bonds would be paid out after the act of expropriation. As if this were not bad enough, in so far as the conservatives and some moderates were concerned, the land reform proposal carried a provision for the forced leasing of property. Goulart withdrew the last two provisions within two months. Nonetheless, this withdrawal, as much as the original presentation of the bill and amendment, were clear indications of political tactics rather than a commitment to economic or ideological purpose. They were also indications of an incipient change in the president's orientation toward a more radical, populist approach. In line with these inclinations, he severed all discussions, however informal, with landowners.

The tenuousness of Jango's solidarity with the positive left on land reform was accentuated by the activities of SUPRA. Following its creation by Congress late in 1962, it began to function in February, 1963, with João Caruso, who had been secretary of agriculture in Brizola's government in Rio Grande do Sul, as its first director. Caruso brought with him substantial experience in dealing with social issues of agriculture, organizing workers, and parcelling out land. Nevertheless, SUPRA activities during the first five months were limited. There was a minimal amount of expropriation, and some effort to establish professorships of rural sociology in agronomy schools -- an activity which to some conservatives smacked of radical political purpose.[23]

Generally, SUPRA was an administrative failure. Caruso complained there was no coherence to the institution, and no presidential interest or support for it. The heterogeneous executive council could not agree on the ground rules for functioning, and the director of the legal department, Fidelino Viana, was a dentist. Frustrated and outraged, Caruso attempted to resign in mid-June. In his letter to Goulart he stressed the lack of cooperation from other government departments:

> While your Excellency defends the necessity and urgency of reform, the Popular Agrarian Institutes retain the contributions they collect, which are destined for SUPRA's disposition. The Minister of Finance has not released a single cruzeiro, even from the budgetary allocation designed for the implementation of /rural/ services. Police sectors /of other government entities/ persecute landless agricultural workers and make it difficult for them to organize.[24]

Caruso was not able, however, to make his resignation immediately effective. He could not personally reach the president; the director of the legal department would not take over the responsibility for SUPRA; and the director of the Department of Rural Publicity and Organization, who might also have taken temporary charge, had not been seen for weeks.[25]

Caruso's difficulties in establishing reasonable
administration within SUPRA reflected a change in the
course of executive agrarian strategy. Concerned about
losing the support of the leftist sections of the PTB and
of organized labor and disillusioned by the failure of
the Three Year plan to deliver to him the support of the
center, Goulart abandoned the positive left. In a major
cabinet reshuffle, he sacrificed Dantas and Furtado, as
well as Almino Afonso and, in a gesture, seemed to rid
himself of military, labor, and financial constraints.
The new cabinet, however, did not inspire any confidence, in spite of the presence of the ex-governor of
São Paulo, Carvalho Pinto as minister of finance. The
weekly magazine, Visão, commented:

> We conclude that if the cabinet /reshuffle/ was intended
> to advance /socio-economic/ reforms, the effort back-
> fired. If the objective was to bring the reform problem
> to an intentional impasse, the president succeeded, for
> he found the ideal scapegoat in congressional resist-
> ance. . . . Besides this cheap Machiavelianism there
> remains the plausible hypothesis that the president wishes
> to transform his role in the impasse into a /merely
> formal interest not backed by serious intentions/. . . , [26]

-- But one, it might be added, which would enable him
to continue capitalizing on the issue.

Populist Politics: End of Conciliation,
June - December, 1963

Gloomily surveying the political scence, the
Correio da Manhã produced the following mid-term as-
sessment in an editorial aptly titled, "Portrait and
Carricature:"

> This is the hour of the degeneration of technical
> problems into political debates, and of political
> debates into military issues. . . . The most con-
> spicuous case is that of agrarian reform. The
> problem is technical. . . . but who mentions that?

> The politicians use agrarian reform as slogans of
> future presidential candidacies. With a total lack
> of knowledge and of ideas, some only wish to main-
> tain the status quo at any price, and others, to
> destroy it, at any cost. Instead of sincere, rea-
> sonable discussion we hear weeping, bellows, shouts.
> And when all this is to no avail, they call on the
> sergeants to make an agrarian reform.[27]

Mildly prophetic, this statement captured some of the
central political concerns of the second half of 1963.
Personal political ambitions and rivalries increasingly diluted the substance of the agrarian issue.
Agrarian reform became a vehicle for demagoguery and
social disorder, a situation which the military
watched with deepening concern. Apparently commited
to a radical constituency which he could not control,
Jango presided over increasing strikes, disorders,
and demonstrations. The activities of Goulart's
brother-in-law, Leonel Brizola, added to the general
tension when he expropriated the American and Foreign
Power Company in Rio Grande do Sul and encouraged rural unionization and land invasion. Inflation was
skyrocketing, and economic activity was at an all
time low. To make matters even worse, the poor har-
vests that had been foreseen months before were resulting in food shortages, hunger, and highly ele-
vated prices for staples. On top of all this, charges
of political corruption were rife, and a congressional investigation of election buying monopolized
newspaper headlines.

The apparent victories of the radical left, consisting of salary increments and greater political
mobilization, caused it to have an inflated perception of its own power and importance, and drove it
to push more forcefully for a complete overhaul of
society. The president, more captive than master of

the radical surge, was swept along on the current, counting on reasonably good relations with the military to carry him through. In this both the extreme left and the president erred in their judgment. Even the legalists and constitutionalists among the military were becoming concerned about the social unrest, which was beginning to affect the enlisted men. Those politicians and military men who had been categorically opposed to Goulart's taking office began to gain new allies, now willing to consider ousting the president as a means of regaining political stability.

Political opposition to Goulart fed on the alienation generated by his increasingly desperate activities. Frustrated by his inability to get his programs enacted, in early October Jango called on Congress to give him decree powers for declaring a state of siege to intervene in Guanabara and São Paulo. He insisted plots were being hatched against him under the leadership of Governor Carlos Lacerda.[28] Jango reconsidered in the wake of strong public reaction within a few days, and the relieved Chamber unanimously approved the presidential message withdrawing the request for a state of siege.[29]

Despite the signs that opposition to him was increasing, Goulart did not abandon his radical tactics. Populist mass mobilization was not merely the basis of Goulart's political support; constant mobilization was his only available threat in bargaining with the opposition. Having maneuvered himself into an impasse, Goulart resorted to the threat of mass unrest and uprising as the only means of influencing the opposition to give in to his programs. With such a narrow constituency whose needs he had to satisfy at least on a symbolic level, Goulart had to stress

incessantly and ever more dramatically his support
for radical social legislation and economic and political reform. For this reason he finally turned to
the strategy of popular agitation to promote agrarian
reform, the focal point of his basic reform program.

SUPRA, under the direction of João Pinheiro Neto
(briefly and unsuccessfully minister of labor in
1962) was ideally suited to this task. As Pinheiro
admitted, SUPRA's objective situation had not changed
in any way after the resignation of Caruso. There
was still no land statute to implement, still no
money, and still no plan. But in the eyes of the new
director these were mere inconveniences. Promising
to "crack this nut" of rural resistance he interpreted
his primary task to be the generation of pressure in
favor of radical agrarian reform, by whatever means
possible.[30] SUPRA's activities until the end of the
year centered on rural labor organization, speech-
making, occasional expropriations, the organization
of demonstrations, and generally whatever measures
would increase rural agitation.[31]

Goulart complemented this strategy with another
attempt to negotiate with Congress. Because of the
division among the political elites and the impasse
in which the presidency found itself Congress acquired an extraordinary importance during the Goulart
term. This importance grew as Goulart's weakness and
political predicament became increasingly apparent.
The fact that Jango could not muster substantial political support outside the legislative arena, and
that political and social groups were polarized and
deadlocked over issues and over Goulart as well, contributed to the increasing Congress's political advantage. It was left to resolve, with a degree of

94

power it did not normally possess, issues that no one
else could or would. Its "increase" in power, was, in
other words, a reflection of the immobility of other
political groups and institutions. Since only Congress could grant Goulart the land reform he wanted,
provided of course, the political rules of the game
did not change, and since passage of agrarian reform
was important for Goulart to legitimize him to the
extreme left, he had no choice but to negotiate with
Congress.

While continuing to support mass mobilization as
a means to threaten his recalcitrant opposition,
within Congress the president's approach became prag-
matically conciliatory and his demands more moderate
than they were in the first half of the year. He
dissociated himself from his brother-in-law, Brizola,
and from his radical policies, and actively worked
for a conciliation of the PSD and PTB positions on
the constitutional amendment. The apparent purpose
of this strategy, which lasted through June and July
was to prevent Chamber approval of the rival Milton
Campos bill, which had passed the Senate in late
1962, and was now being considered by the lower
house. If the bill were passed, it would destroy
Goulart's chance of going down in history as the
father of land reform in Brazil. On August 7, 1963
Goulart achieved this limited aim.

The Campos bill was defeated, but Goulart still
had to secure congressional cooperation, particularly
that of the Chamber, in order to have his own proposals passed. On this score he was not so fortunate.
Following a lull of almost a month in the agrarian
debate, several compromise formulas regarding the
terms of land expropriation were considered. Goulart

95

and the PSD leadership finally settled on a formula
which, when officially made public in the beginning
of September, proved unviable. First, the PSD
representatives from Minas Gerais categorically refused to support any kind of constitutional amendment. Then, the compactos, the ideological wing of
Goulart's own PTB, refused to accept the compromise
package.

So far as the deputies were concerned, more was
at issue than land reform. Both Goulart and the
Congress knew that the president's legitimacy and
credibility were intimately tied to the success of
the reform measures. Also in play was the relative
advantage of the political parties, as each one manipulated the agrarian issue to enhance its own political status both in Congress and in anticipation of
the presidential election. The legislators soon determined that although social unrest was a serious
concern, the executive did not possess an artillery
of believable threats, and did not effectively control the situation. As a consequence Goulart did
little to sway congressional opinion on land reform
in his favor.

Frustrated by this stalemate, Goulart ceased to
dialogue with the legislature. Briefly, at the end
of September, there seemed some possibility that the
president would abandon his withdrawn "contemplative
attitude," and reestablish contact with Congress.[32]
However, in October the original version of the
Goulart-PTB amendment was brought to a vote and
roundly defeated. From October, until Congress' ad-
journment in December, any remaining hope of securing
a viable legislative agrarian package vanished.
Thwarted in its attempt to gain congressional cooper-

ation, the administration gave up any pretense of
concern over political conciliation.

Political Disintegration, December, 1963 - March, 1964

If Goulart made any New Year's resolutions for
1964, one was apparently to abandon all efforts to
work within the system. He left Congress to its own
devices, and concentrated on securing his position on
the radical populist front. In this final phase of
his brief sojourn in the presidency the role of SUPRA
became more important than ever. In particular,
Pinheiro Neto caused grave concern in moderate and
conservative political circles when SUPRA signed an
agreement with the military. The ostensible objective of the agreement was to secure the help of the
armed forces in cadastral surveying. It was becoming clear, however, that as the political impasse
grew the military would exercise a more decisive
political role in the months ahead. Thus, to
Goulart's opposition it seemed as if SUPRA was succeeding only too well in establishing a base of military influence, and perhaps attempting to forestall
unified military opposition to the government. Calling for more stringent criteria for the selection of
administrative personnel, one deputy, incensed over
Pinheiro Neto's behavior and policies, fumed:

> Only this way would we have the conviction that such
> a fundamental sector of state activity /as agriculture/
> has not been handed over to irresponsible professional
> agitators. We absolutely cannot entrust the gigantic
> task of Brazilian agrarian reform to office types,
> divorced from the rural reality, or to a playboy of
> cafe society whose nationalist decisions are stimulated
> by good doses of scotch whiskey in elegant salons or
> in the nightclubs of Copacabana.[33]

Oblivious to charges that his policies and tactics
were divorced from reality, on March 13 Goulart signed two expropriation decrees, one affecting land, the
other affecting private oil refineries. The land decree had originally been announced by Pinheiro in
mid-December. At that time, it stipulated that the
government would have the power to expropriate all
land within thirty kilometers on each side of roads,
wells, and dams. By the time the decree was signed,
the limit was reduced to ten kilometers, a gesture
which did little to sway the opposition in its determination that the time had come for Goulart to part
with his office. The final spark for the revolution
was provided when Jango provoked military insubor-
dination among the rank and file by advocating a
democratization of military procedure. He thus precipitated the wrath of the high command and his evic-
tion from office.

In retrospect, Goulart's abortive efforts to
promote land reform suffered from all the drawbacks
of ad hoc policy. There was little planning, consistency, or coherence to balance the pursuit of short
term populist political objectives. Jango was consequently left playing to a political theater empty
of all but the radical galleries to which he repeatedly appealed. The credibility of his land reform
program suffered as suspicions grew that his campaign
for land reform was fueled by ulterior motives and
devoid of a realistic assessment of the true needs
and problems of Brazilian agriculture. In the view
of the opposition, the mass mobilization and radical
political rhetoric threatened not merely reform, but
chaos. Appalled by the series of strikes, demonstrations, and land invasions, the conservatives were

convinced these were a prelude to a radical person-
alist dictatorship. Goulart's attempt to secure decree powers in October 1963 certainly seemed to point
in this direction.

Under these circumstances the passage of a truly
redistributive agrarian reform within the political
system operating in Brazil in the early 1960s would
have been difficult, at best. Goulart's accession to
the presidency made it altogether impossible.

CASTELO BRANCO AND LAND REFORM

The events of 1964 seem to mark a clear separa-
tion between two distinct eras in Brazilian politics.
Preceding it was the populist democracy of the post-
World War II period; and following, a military dictatorship combining strategies to promote economic
growth with repressive social and political tactics.[34]
Although the government of Castelo Branco unquestionably fell within the latter period and, in fact, inaugurated it, it nevertheless retained in some respects the characteristics of a transitional regime.
The strain of maintaining a semblance of an open
society eventually gave way under the pressures of
economic austerity and political containment. During
his first year and a half in office, however, Castelo
made some attempt to preserve the appearance of civilian government. Primarily, he sought to convey
the impression that he did not wish to redefine com-
pletely the constitution and the political system.
Rather, his purpose was to provide a new sense of
leadership, an elimination of destabilizing extremes
of conduct and ideological expression, and a moral
framework in which democracy could be made to function without threatening the basis of Brazil's

political order. To this end, Castelo combined the
exercise of expanded executive powers with observance of the formalities of the democratic process.
In contrast to the later period of military rule,
continuity with the pre-1964 regime was evident in
the survival of the post-Vargas political party system, and in the continued functioning of governmental
institutions, including the Congress. The government was a civilian-military enterprise, which dealt
with political, economic and social problems in a
decidedly more circumscribed context than that of
the preceding regime, but one which still maintained
elements of bargaining and competition.

This is not to say that the immediate impact of
the Revolution was insubstantial. The radical
"threat" collapsed like a house of cards in the face
of censorship and a massive purge of leftist organizations and populist leadership. Thus, if the political club remained open for business, its membership was altered, and so, by implication, would be
the decisions they arrived at. Furthermore, the rules
of participation were also changed, with a significant effect on the character of policy formation.
The first institutional act of April 9, 1964, besides
increasing the powers of the executive and removing
constitutional obstacles to a purge of the political
leadership, altered the president's relationship to
Congress. The 1946 constitution was formally retained, but the procedure by which Congress considered
legislation was altered. The president acquired the
right to initiate constitutional amendments, which
could now be passed by a simple majority, instead of
the two-thirds vote required previously. Also, Congress was required to act on both amendments and

ordinary legislation within thirty days after the executive submitted the measure. Failure to do so would result in its automatic passage.[35]

Within this framework if the president were to pursue the enactment of a land reform law, he would still have to deal with Congress. However, the provisions of the Institutional Act affecting legislative procedure obviously gave Castelo an advantage not enjoyed by his immediate predecessors, although his powers were not as sweeping as those which were to be exercised by his successors.

The first revolutionary regime carried out an ambitious program of coordinated planning devised by a cabinet of dedicated technocrats under the leadership of Minister of Planning Roberto Campos. Both in his choice of cabinet ministers and in his policy preferences, Castelo was influenced by a group of thinkers from the National War College (Escola Superior da Guerra -- ESG) who, together with a small group of businessmen in Rio de Janeiro, had formed the Institute for Social Research and Study, IPES. Before April 1964, IPES considered political opposition to Goulart to be its first priority. Following the revolution, it provided, through its access to the president, personnel and policy statements and proposals that it had been working on for some period of time.[36] Under the leadership of planning minister Roberto Campos, the cabinet think tank produced a comprehensive program, the Government Program of Action (PAEG), which offered technocratic, capitalist solutions to Brazil's economic problems.[37] It proposed to reduce inflation, which in 1964 reached almost ninety percent, by means of austerity measures whose brunt would be felt principally by the lower class. Its scheme of economic rationalization sought to eliminate inefficient (and frequently traditional) aspects of the economy, introduce capitalism into traditional rural areas, stimulate private industry, and encourage foreign investment.

Among the many problems facing Brazil at this point, land reform was given a high priority, and Castelo made it clear that a land reform law was among his first objectives. Luís Viana Filho recalls that "in the first cabinet meeting of the new government, antagonizing the conservatives who had supported him, Castelo announced the agrarian reform urged by Roberto Campos."[38] There was no lack of documentation, studies, and proposals for land reform at this point. Not only was there a great collection of material from the work of the Milton Campos commission, but IPES as well had conducted a year-long study on the problem in 1963. At the end of that year, it produced a report and a series of proposals, which strongly resembled the Milton Campos bill.[39] Paulo Assis Ribeiro, who was primarily responsible for the project, continued to supervise it until it was finally enacted into law, accompanied by a constitutional amendment. This done, he became the first director of the new Brazilian Institute of Agrarian Reform (IBRA). The fact that Castelo insisted on the passage of a land reform law based on an amendment, and that he succeeded in his purpose within seven months of being in office is no small matter. No one had anticipated that as part of his program the new president would support two laws, one on land reform, and another on housing -- sensitive social issues which contributed so much to the fall of João Goulart.

102

Explanations for Castelo's desire to resolve the agrarian problem could be traced to his sophisticated awareness of the relation between economic and social problems and his first hand experience of rural problems as a native of the state of Ceará in the Northeast. His sensitivity to agrarian problems was no doubt reinforced by his participation in a seminar on agrarian problems at the Joaquim Nabuco Institute of Social Sciences, where he had the opportunity of exchanging ideas with sociologist Gilberto Freyre, Pernambuco governor Miguel Arrais, ligas camponesas head Francisco Julião, and camponês leaders and organizers Fathers Melo and Crespo.[40] Castelo's advisors openly acknowledged that the social unrest of the previous two years had made an impact on the first revolutionary president. In Castelo's view the urgency of an agrarian policy was mandated less by the grievances of Brazil's large rural population than by the fact that an effective agrarian policy was "a sure means of invigorating and stabilizing the entire national economy."[41] He therefore perceived land reform as a means of eliminating some of the causes for social unrest. Finally, in a situation where the masses, both rural and urban, would be particularly hard hit by the austerity program and by the political purge of all organizations tainted by association with Goulart, the agrarian and housing laws, passed in quick succession, were viewed as pacifiers.

The proposals, which remained largely unaltered as a result of discussions preceding their passage, consisted of a constitutional amendment, and an agrarian reform bill. Castelo's amendment (A-10) proposed to do what Jango could not accomplish: alter

103

constitutional provisions affecting the expropriation of property. Like the Goulart-PTB proposal, the
Castelo amendment would permit the payment for expropriated property to be made in bonds redeemable in
twenty years. At variance with the earlier proposals, however, the new administration's measure insured a correction for inflation up to the full value
of the bond. The value of the expropriated property
would be equivalent to its taxable value.

Perhaps the most significant difference between
the two amendments was the use to which each president intended to put it, reflecting distinct policy
objectives. Jango intended to use the expropriation
procedure made available by the amendment as a major
instrument in promoting structural reforms. For him,
the agrarian reform law was pointless without the a-
mendment, and agricultural assistance provisions were
an afterthought to a land policy focusing on the redistribution of property. Castelo, in contrast,
perceived the amendment to be necessary as a means
of providing flexibility and authority to an agrarian
policy, but not as the central focus of that policy.
Not expropriation, but progressive taxation constituted his major instrument of reform. The revolutionary government, unlike its predecessor, did not object to large properties -- only to large unused
properties that could be brought under production,
expropriated, or given over to agroindustry.
Castelo's major objective, in other words, was not a
redefinition of the social structure of rural areas,
but productivity and agricultural development within
a capitalist mode. The only social change in rural
areas contemplated by the Land Statute of 1964 was
the creation of a new group of middle class farmers.

Perhaps the most significant single element shared by
the two presidents' agrarian policies was the conviction that the days of the traditional rural order were
numbered. Their most significant disagreement reflected divergent perceptions of what the new order
should be.

The Passage of the Land Statute

In the formulation of his agrarian policies,
Castelo faced few immediate constraints. His position was not yet compromised by active competition
among the military in preparation for the next presidential contest. Economic difficulties, because
they were not yet compounded by politics, still appeared to be manageable, Congress had been purged of
its leftist elements, including most of the leaders
of the National Liberation Front, and the Institutional Act had facilitated the legislative process
for the president. Within this framework, the agrarian policy initiatives of the president and the
minister of planning proceeded smoothly, although not
without opposition.

The agrarian policy process under Castelo dif-
ferred from that under Goulart in more than formal
institutional contraints. Jango's handling of the
land reform debate was decentralized, and disjointed,
devoid of any visible plan or long term strategy, accompanied by glaring publicity, and aimed primarily
at winning the support of the masses while threatening conservatives generally, and landowners in particular. Also, it was singled out unabashedly as the
keystone of a global attack on the entire political
and social structure. Castelo, on the other hand,
set into motion a process which was carefully planned

and syncronized, controlled, subdued, with a minimum
of media coverage. In contrast to Goulart's thorough
neglect of the "producing classes," and as preparation for legislative approval of the agrarian policy
proposal, Castelo and Campos deliberately and systematically included debates and discussions with the
leadership of these groups. Campos, finance minister
Bulhões, and agriculture minister Hugo Leme frequently commuted to São Paulo to assuage the fears of their
most formidable opposition.[42] In any case, Castelo's
proposals in no sense aimed to destroy the landowners
or launch a frontal attack on the basis of their
power. However, if Goulart overplayed publicity and
general appeals to the public, Castelo did just the
opposite, doing little to gain public understanding
and support through explanatory statements. He expected his plans and their consequences to speak for
themselves. This moratorium on publicity may have
cost him some popular support. But it nevertheless
served an important purpose in preventing a resur-
gence of panic on the part of the landowners.[43]

Despite the fact that Castelo concerned himself
almost immediately with formulating an agrarian policy, the Congress did not interrupt its own activities with respect to this issue. During the months
immediately preceding the revolution, at the point
then the president abandoned any pretense of dialogue with the Congress, a group of deputies in the
Chamber resolved to make another attempt to find a
way out of their deadlock. The Campos bill had been
defeated in the Chamber primarily because of its sponsorship by the UDN, rather than because of tis content. A number of the reformist PSD and UDN deputies
in alliance with Christian Democrats and some other

groups, reasoned that if a bill with a neutral sponsorship were to be introduced, it stood a good chance of securing some PTB support and therefore of passage. The enactment of an agrarian bill at this time was perceived as a means of preempting the possible implementation of Goulart's more radical designs. Accordingly, Christian Democrat Aniz Badra was induced to act as sponsor of the new bill, which appeared to be a more schematic, more poorly drafted version of the Campos bill. After the revolution, spurred by the threat implicit in Castelo's announcement of his own reform program, the Chamber passed the bill on April 7, 1964.

If passage of the bill by the Chamber was intended to forestall Castelo's presentation of his own land reform proposal, the strategy failed. In total disregard of what was already proposed or voted, the president introduced his own bill in the last days of April. Under the guidance of Paulo Assis Ribeiro, and in constant contact with Roberto Campos, the agrarian reform work group in the ministry of planning reviewed past legislation and drafted an agrarian reform bill heavily based on the IPES project drawn up earlier by Assis Ribeiro, which in turn relied on the Campos bill. The drafting of a constitutional amendment affecting the terms of expropriation was entrusted to Milton Campos following a similar process of discussion.[44] By the second week in May the proposal was ready for wider debate.

Unlike the previous regime, which lacked a defined plan of action, the Castelo government had mapped out a careful strategy for its proposal. The first step was to assuage the sore feelings of the landowners who not only had borne the brunt of the

radical attack by the previous regime, but who had
also cooperated in deposing it. Accordingly, the
first consultation outside executive circles was with
representatives of the Brazilian Rural Confederation
(CRB).[45] The study group coordinator also met with a
conference of the state agrarian federations. Concurrently, there were meetings with a representative
of the Federation of Rural Workers of the State of
São Paulo (FARESPE), of the National Union of Cooperatives, and with economists from the ministries of
planning and agriculture.

The landowners' organization submitted a total
of forty-four amendments to the proposal, of which
forty were adopted. Members of both the CRB (in
interviews) and of the administration seemed to agree
that the changes accepted were not crucial, and that
on all truly essential points, Roberto Campos, who
made himself readily available to the CRB, remained
aimable but steadfastly unmoved. Although the landowners, like other employer groups, did not have a
decisive voice, the ruralists were pleased to be consulted and have their opinions taken into account and
at least partially incorporated. The CRB was not,
however, speaking for all the landowners -- a fact
which explains subsequent landowner opposition to the
measure. The staunchest defenders of the old order
were not necessarily members of the confederation.

Following these preliminary consultations with
the leadership of important social sectors and the
approval of a new draft of the legislation by Roberto
Campos, the bill was ready for limited circulation
in a wider political circle as a restricted document.
At this second stage, beginning the first of June,
the circle of debate was widened to include Senate

and Chamber leaders, the leadership of political parties, the Brazilian Rural Confederation, rural workers confederations, and state secretaries of agriculture. These consultations, made as a good will gesture by the government, did not have an appreciable impact on the bill. More influential was the president's personal review of the drafts of the bill and amendment. Further discussion with party leaders in Congress was delayed for the remainder of the month by petitions from paulista "producing classes," who requested further meetings with the work group and the president.

When the first of the meetings with congressional leaders was held on June 29, it became clear that congressional opposition, or more precisely, the UDN, (supposedly the government's "own" party) constituted the major obstacle to the passage of the amendment and law. The UDN leaders, including such social policy hard liners as Senator Daniel Krieger and Deputies Bilac Pinto and Ernani Sátiro, arrived with their own advisors, among them, Antônio Delfim Neto, who was to become minister of finance in 1967 under Costa e Silva and financial wizard of the revolution. The undenistas declared that they "considered the bill totally unacceptable for debate " and that they would "present their own substitute within thirty days."[46]

In comparison to the UDN, the PSD, with which the agrarian study group and Roberto Campos met next, seemed eminently more reasonable, maintaining an attitude of "constructive criticism," on both amendment and bill. The old politicians' party was, as usual, playing the accommodationist game. The PSD delegation, led by Amaral Peixoto, Gileno de Carli (who had drafted an agrarian bill of his own in 1962), and

Guilhermino de Oliveira, met several times with the group from July 2 to July 7.[47] Consultations with other parties followed. In none of these activities did the PTB appear to assume an important role.

Further discussions of the agrarian proposals were postponed for a short time awaiting the UDN substitute proposals. These never materialized. Concurrently, a meeting of state secretaries of agriculture in Viçosa, Minas Gerais from July 28 to 31 highlighted the agrarian issue and generated considerable publicity, while in substance affecting the proposal only marginally with suggested amendments and substitutes.[48] During August the bills underwent several more drafts. The tenth draft of the bill, which was submitted again for presidential perusal, reflected an important alteration. It no longer contained an amendment establishing a system of rural justice. The major veto apparently came from Milton Campos, then minister of justice, who adopted a decidedly conservative position in contrast to his sporting reformism during the Goulart period.[49]

During the subsequent slow waiting period, which dragged on into October, "educational" meetings on agrarian policy continued to be held. Roberto Campos devoted a great deal of time to addressing various groups, including what remained of rural unions in Recife. His activities also included lengthy sessions with the Chamber where the greater part of dissent and discussion was motivated by the still recalcitrant UDN leadership. The compromises exacted by the undenistas in exchange for withdrawing their opposition appeared to include essential modifications on the location of taxing authority, on the final value of land reform bonds, and on the rate of the

110

progressive taxation on idle` land.[50]

The last week of October marked the final stage
of the process of bringing a policy of land reform
into being. On October 21, legislative consideration
of the amendment was initiated in a special joint
session required to reach a decision on the issue in
thirty days. The land bill was submitted a few days
later, on October 26. The careful and elaborate
strategies pursued prior to the formal presentation
of the measures to Congress no doubt aided considerably in smoothing the way to the acceptance of the
bill, but by no means succeeded in eliminating all
obstacles. Obviously prepared for this type of contingency, the minister of planning had his crew of
consultants constantly on hand during the prolonged
daily sessions until the measures had actually
passed.

The major center of opposition was from the
die-hard conservatives and the UDN in particular.
The most conservative deputies expressed embittered
outrage over what appeared to be a continuation of
Goulart's policy. Others protested the impropriety
of voting on the administration's measures while the
Badra bill was presumably still under discussion.
In the final days prior to the vote, the difficulties
appeared to multiply rather than diminish. The UDN
reporter of the special commission, Pacheco Chaves,
resigned for reasons of total disagreement with the
reformist measures. No ready substitute to fill his
place could be found in either the UDN or the PSD.
The government finally appealed to the "opposition"
and convinced Senator Aurélio Viana, a member of the
Brazilian Socialist Party, to undertake the responsibility of reporting on the measures to the joint

111

session of Congress. In its review of the legislation and the 436 amendments submitted by the UDN,
support for the agrarian task force came primarily
-- and ironically -- from the opposition, i.e., the
PTB, Christian Democrats, Socialists, and other minor
parties, all of which had been heavily purged. However, as Goulart had discovered earlier, these votes
alone were insufficient for the passage of the measures. Until the eve of the balloting the UDN leadership insisted on remaining in the opposition. At the
last moment, however, following a meeting with the
president, João Mendes urged the UDN legislators to
vote as they individually saw fit. In the final analysis, it would appear that the party leaders felt
it politically more expedient to contribute to having
the national Congress pass the law than to see the
legislation approved automatically as a result of
congressional inaction. As a result, both Amendment
No. 10, modifying articles 141 and 146, section 16 of
the constitution and the Land Statute were passed by
joint session of both houses of Congress. The amendment was approved on November 6, 1964. Only thirty-
three deputies and two senators remained "guardians
of democracy," as Deputy Último de Carvalho (PSD-
Minas Gerais) put it with great sadness, and voted
against it.

The Land Statute was destined to be the high
point of land reform experience in Brazil. Several
unique reasons explain the enactment of the reform
measures at this time. First, President Castelo
Branco accorded them top priority and his consistent
and unequivocal personal support. Second, Institutional Act No. 1 have the executive ascendancy over
Congress in the legislative process. Finally, despite

some strong residual suspicions, the UDN and other anti-Goulart groups felt more secure about land reform in Castelo's hands than in those of his predecessor. Castelo's personal preoccupation with socioeconomic reform was a luxury he could afford as long as the political, military, and economic problems did not become pressing. Shortly thereafter his attention became wholly absorbed by problems in his economic stabilization program. In the effort to impose economic stability, the niceties of social reform and democracy were pushed aside. If Castelo had not achieved the passage of the agrarian measures before 1965, he might not have been able to do so afterwards. As chapter 6 explains, the social impact of the legislation has in any case been minimal. Its enactment provided no automatic means of implementation and Castelo's successors have not shared his vision of social justice for the rural masses as a key to Brazil's economic stability.

NOTES

1. Needless to say, there were countless lesser proposals dealing with particular aspects of agriculture and with details of bills, as well as bills and decrees aimed at explaining and implementing previously discussed or enacted measures. A review of these measures would not contribute materially to understanding the agrarian debate.

2. Quadros, in his short time in office, left behind a record of concern for agriculure. In addition to creating a commision to study agrarian reform, he called into being an "Executive Coordinating Group for Rural Credit" and enhanced the availability of credit for agricultural production. JB, May 28, 1961, p. 11.

3. The new commission was composed of prominent national figures who were selected for their expertise in agricultural matters. The members of the Special Commission for Agrarian Reform were Milton Campos, UDN leader, statesman, former gover-

nor of Minas Gerais, and coordinator of the commission; Deputies Nestor Duarte and Barbosa Lima Sobrinho; Bishop Dom Fernando Gomez of Goiânia; Inâcio Rangel, Osvaldo Guzmão, and Jader Andrade of SUDENE, the Superintendancy for the Development of the Northeast; Rômulo de Almeida; Tomaz Pompeu de Accioly Borges, United Nations Food and Agricultural Organization (FAO); João Napoleao de Andrade, Brazilian Association of Rural Agricultural Credit, ABCAR; Ernani Maia and Ivã Luz, National Institute of Immigration and Colonization, INIC; Dom Helder Câmara, Bishop of Recife; and Edgar Teixeira Leite, of the Brazilian Rural Confederation, the landowners association. JB, May 20, 1961, 1/4, and August 15, 1961, 8/7,8. Also see Visão, April 28, 1961, p.14.

4. Osny Duarte Pereira, A Constituição Federal e Suas Modificações Incorporadas ao Texto (Rio de Janeiro: Civilização Brasileira, 1966).

5. ICOPS, Brazil Election Factbook (Washington, D.C.: Operations and Policy Research, 1965), p.84.

6. An absolute majority in each state assembly is required to merit approval. The proposal subsequently has to receive an absolute majority in two separate sessions (i.e., one year apart) in both houses, or a two-thirds majority in a single session in each house.

7. Ronald M. Schneider, The Political System of Brazil, pp. 83, 84. Even labor, which had been Goulart's primary constituency from the early fifties when he was made Vargas' minister of labor, was showing signs of independent behavior, calling into question Goulart's paternalistic assumptions in his relations with workers. Kenneth Erickson develops this point in his The Brazilian Corporative State and Working Class Politics.

8. Cf. Skidmore, pp. 266-267; Schneider, p.83.

9. Schneider, p.83.

10. Visão, February 17, 1961, p.13.

11. Ibid., February 24, 1961, p.15.

12. JB., December 31, 1961.

13. Politics in Brazil, p. 218.

14. Pernambuco had a territorial tax proposal before the state assembly in November 1961. JB, November 8, 1961, p.5.

114

15. Even the pretender to the nonexistent Brazilian throne, Prince João de Orleans e Bragança publicly endorsed a "balanced" land reform, but indicated strong disapproval of the "....demagogic activities of the ligas camponesas. JB, April 28, 1962, p.1.

16. Diario de São Paulo, May 2, 1961.

17. In its report on the meeting, Visão carried a photograph of the governors, with a caption that read, "Gathered in Araxá, the governors limited themselves to repeating what has already been said." June 15, 1962, p.18.

18. Among the signers were Arraes, Pernambuco; Ney Braga, Paraná; Brizola, Rio Grande do Sul; and Mauro Borges, Goiás.

19. Visão, February 2, 1962, p.13, and JB, January 26, 1962, p. 5.

20. Explanation by Furtado to Correio da Manhã, April 1, 1963, p. 1.

21. CM, March 22, 1963, p.6.

22. Ibid., May 19, 1963, p.6.

23. See, for instance, CM, June 13, 1963 on SUPRA expropriation of land in Paracambí and Campos in Rio de Janeiro state, and in the Vale do Rio Maranhão in Goias.

24. CM, June 14, 1963, Canderno 2, p.1.

25. CM, June 18, 1963, p.3.

26. Visão, June 28, 1963.

27. May 12, 1963, p.6. This last is a reference to the appeal made by Brizola to the military of Natal the preceding week.

28. Ibid., October 5, 1963, p.1. As it turned out, in the long run he was not entirely mistaken. The two cities played an important part in coordinating the opposition movement which eventually deposed him.

29. CM, October 8, 1963, p.1.

30. Ibid., August 17, 1963, p.2; July 10, 1963, p.10; June 28, 1963, p.2.

31. There is a resemblance between SUPRA, and its Chilean counterpart, INDAP. INDAP, under the direction of Jacques

Chonchol, was charged with communist infiltration and deliberate agitation in the countryside. Cf., Robert Kaufman, The Politics of Land Reform in Chile, 1950-1970. Public Policy, Political Institutions, and Social Change (Cambridge, Massachusetts: Harvard University Press, 1972), pp. 102-103.

32. CM, September 25, 1963, p.6.

33. Anais da Câmara, I, 1963/1964, 12 session, January 12, 1964. Cited hereafter as Anais.

34. For a review of this period see Schneider, The Political System of Brazil; Luís Viana Filho, O Govêrno Castelo Branco (Rio de Janeiro: Livraria José Olympio, 1975); Riordan Roett, editor, Brazil in the Sixties (Nashville, Tenn.: Vanderbilt University Press, 1972); Alfred Stepan, editor, Authoritarian Brazil (New Haven: Yale University Press, 1973); and Georges-André Fiechter, Brazil since 1964: Modernization Under a Military Regime (New York: John Wiley, 1975).

35. A complete compilation of the 1946 constitution, with all amendments, institutional acts and complimentary acts up to 1966 can be found in Osny Duarte Pereira, A Constituição Federal e suas Modificações Incorporadas ao Texto (Rio de Janeiro: Civilização Brasileira, 1966).

36. Affiliates of IPES who found their way into the service of the Castelo government included: Roberto Campos, Minister of Planning; Octavio Bulhões, Minister of Finance; Luís Viana Filho, Chief of the Civilian Household; Garrido Tôrres, Director of the National Institute of Economic Development; General Golbery de Couto e Silva, Director of the National Information (security) Service. Source: IPES files.

37. On the economic policies of the military government see Albert Fishlow, "Some Reflections on Post-1964 Brazilian Economic Policy," in Stepan; Ministério do Planejamento e Coordenação Econômica, Programa de Ação Econômica do Govêrno, 1964-1966 (Rio de Janeiro, 1964); Celso Furtado, Análise do Modelo Brasileiro (Rio de Janeiro: Civilização Brasileira, 1972); and Mário Enrique Simonsen, A Nôva Economia Brasileira (Rio de Janeiro: Livraria José Olympio, 1974).

38. O Govêrno Castelo Branco, p. 274.

39. The report was published in 1964 as: A Reforma Agrária: Problemas, Bases, e Soluções.

40. Viana Filho, p. 274.

41. Ibid., p. 262.

42. Ibid., pp. 263, 264.

43. Congressional debates, newspapers, and journals, which
had been excellent sources for the reconstruction of the land
reform debate under Goulart were poor sources on this issue
after April 164, both because of the absence of publicity by
the government and increased repression and censorship. Besides relying, where possible, on these standard sources, I
have reconstructed the passage of the Land Statute from
numerous interviews conducted with persons directly involved --
politicians, cabinet ministers, and administrators -- and from
a particularly useful report written by Paulo Assis Ribeiro
describing in minute detail the passage of Amendment No. 10
and of the Land Statute: "Implantação da Reforma Agrária.
Relatório de Abril 1964 -- Março 1967," (Rio de Janeiro, 1967,
mimeo). Luís Viana Filho's chapter on agrarian policy in his
book on the Castelo government is a somewhat superficial treatment of the subject. It offers a few otherwise unpublished
details of the period based on personal correspondence and
observation from his vantage point as Chief of the Civilian
Household. Its treatment of the struggle over issues is unfortunately uninformative.

44. Ibid., p. 276.

45. Particularly with Eudes de Souza Leão Pinto, José Resende
Peres, Durval Garcia de Menezes, and Edgar Teixeira Leite.

46. Assis Ribeiro, "Implantação," p.3.

47. Ibid.

48. Ibid., p.4.

49. Ibid., p.6.

50. Ibid., p.7.

4. The Congressional Debate: Legislative Politics and the Policy Process

Historically, Latin American legislatures have neither enjoyed stability of existence nor consistency of institutional integrity. Whenever they have attempted decisive structural reforms of their nations' social and economic systems, powerful conservative elites have repeatedly conspired to overturn them in favor of centralized authoritarian rule. During the periods when it has been in existence, the Brazilian Congress has generally been considered more powerful than those of its Spanish speaking neighbors. It too, however, has been subject to periodic subordination and suspension by authoritarian regimes. In the course of those highly centralized intervals, when the Congress has functioned at all, such as during the Vargas dictatorship and the present military government, it has been reduced to a rubber stamp.

Because of the persistence of regional power, the Brazilian Congress has had the ability to reassert itself. Regional interests have historically found most prominent expression in the Congress and in a functioning federal system. The Old Republic (1889-1930), dominated by the "politics of the governors," and the Second Republic (1946-1964) were characterized by strong state and regional political

influence. Some of the major efforts of both the
Vargas dictatorship and the present military regime
have, in fact, concentrated on curbing the independent political expression found at the state level
and manifested in the Congress.

In addition to providing a direct avenue of expression for regional interests, the Brazilian legislature has also served another important purpose.
With the expansion of suffrage in the twentieth century it has functioned as an arena for the expression
of newly mobilized political groups. The politics of
mass mobilization created opportunities for populist
political leaders to organize new constituencies as
a basis for political careerism. Although these political actors more often than not represented their
own interests rather than the interests of their constituencies, they nevertheless promoted popular reformist issues as a means of creating a broader base
of power. Thus, a politics of symbolism rather than
substance came to dominate congressional behavior.

A careful examination of congressional behavior
in reference to the highly charged land reform issue
can yield some valuable insights into how various
elements of the Brazilian political system responded
to the threat of basic social reform. Particularly
during the unrestrained "democratic" period of
Goulart, an examination of congressional activity reveals the full spectrum of ideological and institutional conflict over basic reforms. Since the legislature is an official forum, the attitudes and strategies of political parties and groups remain a matter
of public record to a greater extent than in the
absence of legislative activity. This permits a more
careful scrutiny than might otherwise be possible of

attitudes expressed and positions taken on a given issue.

The fact that the land reform issue spans two political periods divided by the 1964 revolution permits the study of the influence of the Congress under distinct circumstances. Clearly, the survival of some congressional independence into the Castelo period enhances the comparability of congressional activity under the two regimes. Political party behavior and attitudes can thus be traced and compared for programmatic and ideological consistency or, by contrast, for political opportunism.

Finally, legislative behavior can be assessed in relation to more immediate political circumstances and, most particularly, in terms of the conduct of the presidency and the degree of consensus among national elites. Weakness or indecision on the part of the executive has invariably resulted in an increase of congressional leverage. Precisely this type of situation prevailed under João Goulart. He assumed power in the midst of a crisis and in the face of considerable political and military opposition. His subsequent need to rely on left wing populism in the absence of firm support from the military and major economic and social interests only aggravated his problems. During the Goulart administration, executive power was circumscribed not only by the formal institutional arrangements of representative democracy, but also by immediate political circumstances. The land reform issue thus provides an opportunity to examine congressional behavior, if not at its best, at least at its strongest.

The Castelo period, in contrast, is characterized by a decidedly more unified elite and also by an

executive who, whatever his popularity, enjoyed considerable respect, and the crucial support of strategic economic and political elites. For these as
well as institutional reasons, the scope of congressional activity was more limited.

The following examination of the Brazilian Congress is divided into two parts. This chapter will
detail the struggle between the president and Congress over agrarian policy from the point of view of
the latter. The next chapter will take a closer look
at the behavior of legislators for the purpose of
analyzing the interaction of ideology, interests, and
opportunism in political behavior.

As noted earlier, bills introduced by the president must first be considered by the Chamber of Deputies. If approved by the lower house, they are
brought before the Senate. Since Goulart's agrarian
proposals never reached this point, the Chamber will
be the major focus of this discussion.

POLITICAL PARTIES AND INTEREST REPRESENTATION

The political party system which functioned until 1965, and which continues to exist under the
cover of the present two official parties, came into
being in 1945 when Getúlio Vargas stepped down from
power after a fifteen year sojourn in the presidency.
Three major parties, as well as a number of small
ones, came into existence. Of the larger ones, the
National Democratic Union, UDN, had brought together
the opposition to Vargas, and was based on a heterogeneous coalition of social groups The other two
major parties, the Social Democratic Party, PSD, and
the Brazilian Labor Party, PTB, were both created by

Table 4-1

BRAZILIAN POLITICAL PARTIES, 1945-1964

Political Party	Initials	Translation
Partido de Representação Popular	PRP	Popular Representation Party
Partido Republicano	PR	Republican Party
Partido Social Progressista	PSP	Social Progressive Party
Partido Liberal	PL	Liberal Party
União Democrática Nacional	UDN	National Democratic Union
Partido Social Democrático	PSD	Social Democratic Party
Partido Democrata Cristão	PDC	Christian Democratic Party
Partido Trabalhista Brasileiro	PTB	Brazilian Labor Party
Partido Trabalhista Nacional	PTN	National Labor Party
Partido Social Trabalhista	PST	Social Labor Party
Partido Socialista Brasileiro*	PSB	Brazilian Socialist Party
Partido Comunista Brasileiro*	PCB	Brazilian Communist Party
Movimento Trabalhista Renovador	MTR	Labor Renovation Movement
Partido Ruralista Brasileiro**	PRB	Brazilian Ruralist Party
Partido Orientador Trabalhista**	POT	Orienting Labor Party
Partido de Boa Vontade	PBV	Good Will Party

* Illegal as of 1948

** Cancelled following 1950 elections because of insufficient votes.

123

Vargas himself. The origins of the PTB can be traced
back to the Estado Nôvo phase of the Vargas dictatorship, when labor was organized to serve as a personal
vehicle for the president. The PSD was formed out of
the state political machines that had functioned during the old Republic, and on which Vargas built his
government. Essentially a "politicians party,"[1] it
was an organization of political in-groups, whose
primary interest was that of maintaining themselves
in office.

Of all the parties, only the PSD, PTB, and UDN
enjoyed a nation-wide base, which in no way implied
ideological consistency or programmatic uniformity.
The primary attraction these parties held out for the
electorate was that of personalities rather than principles. Ideological and programmatic inconsistency
was manifest in indiscriminate alliances and the irrelevance of party platforms to the character and
interests of constituencies. State sections of a
party frequently found themselves contradicting each
other as well as the national leadership. Parties
allied at the national level or in one state could be
in bitter opposition in another.

Since the primary functions of the party system
were political control and elite recruitment, not representation, these characteristics might not have
been a serious shortcoming from a system maintenance
point of view. Indeed the clientelistic-patrimonial
relationship of politicians to the electorate on one
hand, and the emotional and vaguely nationalistic
populism on the other are perfectly logical from this
perspective.

However expedient, this system bore the seeds of
its own destruction. The growing electorate --

124

particularly in urban areas -- generated a race among parties for new constituencies. In the long run, the concurrent strategies of mass mobilization to create new electoral constituencies, and elite control to contain the latter's reformist expectations were contradictory and created tensions in the functioning of the political system. The political system was unable to absorb successfully the rapid social mobilization that had taken place. Thus it was becoming clear that populism was getting out of hand and beginning to threaten the stability of clientelism as a control mechanism. This is particularly evident in the distribution of seats by party in the two houses of Congress. Table 4-2 indicates that in the 1945 to 1964 period, two important changes occurred. First, among the three major parties, the net balance shifted from the traditional and clientelistically based PSD and UDN and toward the more populistically inclined PTB in both houses of Congress. Second, although the three major parties managed to retain a constant percentage of the seats in the Senate, their combined share in the Chamber of Deputies dropped 10.4 percent.

The gains of the PTB and the minor parties signaled a threat to the clientelistic basis of politics in Brazil and to elite control. The accession of Goulart to the presidency dramatically emphasized the dangers of this process to the strategic elites. Deprived of their support, Goulart relied almost exclusively on an increasingly radical populist strategy. To make matters worse, as a result of six deputies switching parties, the PTB in 1963 became the majority party in the Chamber for the first time, casting it in a leadership role in the lower house,

Table 4-2

DISTRIBUTION OF CONGRESSIONAL SEATS BY PARTY, 1954-1960

	1945	%	1950	%	1955	%	1960	%	% Net shift
Senate: total seats	42	100	63	100	63	100	63	100	
PSD..........	26	61.9	28	44.4	23	36.5	21	33.3	-28.6
UDN..........	10	23.8	11	17.5	13	20.6	19	30.2	+ 6.4
PTB..........	2	4.8	5	7.9	16	25.4	17	27.0	+22.2
3 major parties...	38	90.5	44	69.8	52	82.5	57	90.5	0
Others.........	4	9.5	19	30.2	11	17.5	6	9.5	0
Chamber: total seats	286	100	304	100	326	100	326	100	
PSD..........	151	52.8	93	30.6	114	35.0	115	35.3	-17.5
UDN..........	77	26.9	54	17.8	74	22.7	70	21.5	- 5.4
PTB..........	22	7.7	43	14.1	56	17.2	66	20.2	+12.5
3 major parties...	250	87.4	190	62.5	244	74.9	251	23.0	-64.4
Others.........	36	12.6	114	37.5	82	25.1	75	77.0	+64.4

Source: Adaptation of Table 5 in Marta Cehelsky, "A Case Study in Urbanization: Brazil" in Philip B. Taylor and Sam Schulman, eds. Population and Urbanization Problems in Latin America, University of Houston, 1971, p.68.

and giving it greater leverage over committee business. The populist trend gave credence to the fears
of conservatives that political stability was about
to be engulfed by a populist wave.

Curiously, the actual effect of populism on
Brazilian politics was somewhat ambiguous. Populism
did succeed in mobilizing more people into the political arena and at a greater rate than the elistist
and statist political system could absorb without
endangering its stability. Thus, from their perspective, conservative elites may have been correct in
fearing this phenomenon's potential for the prevailing social order. Their perceptions, however, of the
ideological importance of the threat were misplaced.
Populism was ideologically oriented only presumptive-
ly and indirectly by serving as a political procedure
for the incorporation of the masses. Since the masses
and the issues of their oppression and rights were
consistently identified with radical leftist programs, the ideological inference was easy to make.
In actual fact, however, although vaguely nationalistic and reformist, populism was not particularly
more expressive of ideologies and interests than was
clientelism. Acting as often to obfuscate as to clarify issues and interests, neither populism nor clientelism served as effective vehicles for the articulation of competing class and group demands. Consequently, Brazilian elections mobilized the electorate
without producing outcomes which significantly dis-
criminated among specific group needs and interests
according to party ideology.

A possible alternative route for interest expression bypassing the electoral process might have
been the use of lobbies and pressure groups to influ-

127

ence legislators directly. In fact, my analysis of
the land reform issue indicates that social and economic organizations in Brazil are poor articulators
or interests, especially before Congress.[2] The corporatist and clientelistic organization of social and
economic groups causes its members to direct the bulk
of their attention to the executive, who can be count-
ed on to deliver the desired pay offs. In his study
of interest group behavior in Brazil, Schmitter observes that to the extent that an interest group fo-
cuses on the Congress, its target is more likely to
be an individual congressman with whom, presumably, a
preexisting clientelistic relationship obtains rather
than the objective working commission which reviews
pending legislation. Group activity might in this
sense be described as being generally person oriented
rather than issue oriented. This observation is
borne out in my study of the discussion of land reform. Groups concerned with this issue would send
letters, messages, and telegrams to individual deputies. These, in turn, would read the communications
into the legislative record and consider their obligation fulfilled. Congressmen do not, with some exceptions, see themselves as representatives of specific interests.

Until the early sixties, individual appeals constituted the full extent of pressure activity by economic interests in Congress. Then, at least to a limited degree, a more organized attempt at pressure
group activity became apparent. Two highly organized
pressure groups came into being with heavy industrial
financial backing, as well as support from foreign
business firms. The first of these groups, the

Brazilian Institute for Democratic Action, IBAD, was
founded in 1959 for the declared purpose of "defending democracy."[3] The other organization, the Institute of Social Research and Study, IPES, came into
being in 1962, also supported by industry and a sector of the military. Its obstensible purpose was to
study national problems and their relationship to
democratic principles.[4] Both groups claimed to have
been inspired by the Alliance for Progress and the
encyclicals of Pope John XXIII.

Well publicized congressional investigations of
the two organizations revealed that altruism was perhaps not the main motivation for IPES and IBAD, and
that their activities were not politically innocuous.
IBAD was charged with "tampering with elections, and
corruption of the press, politicians, and authorities
through internal and external resources."[5] Although
the congressional investigation could not actually
prove that IPES was guilty of similar activities,
there is evidence that suggests this organization was
no less innocent of such charges.[6]

Of greater interest is the decision made by
these two organizations to establish themselves in
the Chamber of Deputies with consultants, aids, mi-
crophones, telephones, and a working budget. Of the
two organizations, IPES seems to have been more active and also more directly responsible for the tasks
of buttonholing legislators, and lining up support
for IPES sponsored bills.[7] By March 1963, IPES had
submitted 24 bills through "its" deputies.

Although it cannot be said that IPES ever acquired anything approaching a controlling influence
in the Chamber, it at least enjoyed close ties with
such leaders of the conservative democratic Parlia-

mentary Action bloc in the lower house as João Mendes
and Raymundo Padilha. Another aspect of its special
leverage in Congress originated in its research functions. IPES systematically concerned itself with the
preparation of studies on major issues under consideration by the president and Congress. Among its
most important studies was that of agrarian reform.
Although it failed to have a bill of its own introduced in the legislature, its agrarian reform study
ultimately served as a working document for the elaboration of the Land Statute.

LEGISLATING LAND REFORM: JOÃO GOULART

That an institutional crisis was at the heart of
the debate on structural reforms seemed fairly clear
to members of the politically aware public. Visão
cogently pointed out that this crisis could be traced
at least to Jânio Quadros' resignation in 1962. The
leadership vacuum, the article noted, had not been
filled since then, with a resulting absence of ade-
quate authority to confront critical decisions.

> In political epoques such as ours, there is no one
> with this authority and this power. It is point-
> less to speak of coherent economic policy when the
> major political and economic problem, the issue of
> income redistribution. . . , is not conducted with
> real authority /derived from/ free consent from
> below. . . . The left, as much as the right, has no
> faith in the efficacy of the Brazilian political
> class. . . . [8]

João Goulart himself was particularly anxious to resolve this crisis of immobility, not the least for his
own sake. Congress too was beginning to feel the
pressure of public opprobrium. Typically, the media
lamented that at a time when the country was in des-

perate need of a variety of reform measures, the national legislature contented itself with being nothing more than "a simple machine for obtaining favors."[9] Newspapers admonished the national legislators that Congress would be left behind, obsolete and disgraced, as the rest of the nation, with the President in the lead, embarked on an ambitious program of social reforms. These reproaches seems finally to affect some of the legislators. In a typical remark, a Deputy from Pernambuco declared that "instead of discussing the gender of angels and the allocation of minor posts," Congress ought to get to work considering such substantive policy proposals as agrarian reform.[10]

It seemed fairly clear to most national legislators that the time was fast approaching when some sort of agrarian legislation would be passed. The real bone of contention and the point that was to cause polarization and heated argument were the pivotal issues of what really constituted land reform and how it was to be carried out. Those who were arguing for land reform, in the root meaning of the term, insisted that only a total revision of the land tenure system through expropriation of latifundia and redistribution to the landless or to minifundia owners could solve the social and economic problems of the countryside. But such a program of expropriation would ultimately require that the constitution be amended to permit expropriation of land and payment for it in bonds redeemable after a number of years had elapsed. Consequently, to these partisans, the cause of the agrarian controversy could be reduced to the problem of the constitutional amendment. But the issue was much more complex than just a simple choice between altering the constitution, or retaining the standing provisions requiring prior payment in cash for expropriated land. There were several subsidiary issues, such as the degree of correction for inflation to be permitted in the case of agrarian bonds; the definition of a latifundium; the specification of which level of government would have powers to tax the land (município, state government, or federal government); and the rate of taxation on unproductive land.

Other dilemmas surfaced to further complicate the issue. Ideological positions were by no means the only stakes in the debate. Of no small consequence was the challenge to the president's legitimacy to govern and establish policy. Similarly at issue were the positions and careers of a number of deputies whose power base lay in the countryside. At another level of consideration there was the strategic problem of relative gains. Each party, and each deputy, when asked to consider a presidential proposal, addressed not only the objective merits of the measure, but also its political and electoral consequences. The progress and success of political careers depended on tactical victories that would increase access to clientelistic payoffs or enhance the position of a given political actor or group in the populist struggle at the polls. Thus, presidential candidates and party factions fastened on agrarian reform as an issue with high visibility and good potential for enhancing their own positions. It was the president's task to forge out of this material a block of alliances capable of furnishing the support he needed for his own political goals.

Phase I: Agrarian Policy and Congressional Strategies

For the legislature and for political parties, as for the president, the parlimentary experiment of 1962 was a period of indecision, a time of taking stock, and in general, the calm before the storm. The formal limitations of parliamentary government made any interaction between the executive and legislative branches unfruitful for the resolution of problems. There was general dissatisfaction with the current institutional arrangement, and an uncertainty fed by the knowledge that they would be revised by a plebiscite at some point in the near future. Consequently, the foremost political concerns of all politicians were the plebiscite on the one hand, and on the other, the congressional elections of October 1962 which would determine the party balance in Congress with which Goulart would deal for most of his term.

As pointed out earlier in the discussion of presidential policy, Goulart's strategy for this period was to do everything in his power to ensure an early plebiscite. For this reason, his public statements and political tactics were deliberately restrained, and leaned toward conservatism. Presumably to make himself as non-controversial as possible to political moderates and conservatives the president did not become centrally involved in the October elections. He had already presented his plan of Basic Reforms (agrarian, tax, administrative, fiscal, educational reforms) to the country, but was careful not to appear too radical or too insistent.

Congress and the political parties were facing a somewhat different set of problems in regard to

133

basic reforms. If Goulart's need was to tone down
a radical image, that of Congress, or more particularly of the two large conservative parties, the UDN
and the PSD, was to live down the accusations made
in the press that their immobilism was responsible
for the social turmoil and policy impasse. Their
strategy was to come out clearly in favor of structural reforms in a series of declarations made from
late 1961 through mid-1962.

The objective reasons for the pro-reform unanimity were easily apparent. Some sort of national
policy would, it was expected, bring under control
the radicalizing tendencies spontaneously appearing
in the countryside: ligas camponesas led by a
man clearly sympathetic to the views of Fidel
Castro; rural unions organized by the Catholic
church, and by the Communist Party; land invasions; and even attempts by individual states to deal
with agrarian problems in moderate (São Paulo under
Carvalho Pinto) or radical (Rio Grande do Sul
under Brizola) fashion.

But there were other reasons as well. It was
easy enough for congressmen and their parties to be
in favor of "reforms" when they were innocuous, or
when their exact provisions were not spelled out. In
such circumstances a pro-reform position could only
enhance one's political appeal. It was another matter to approve a series of specific proposals potentially threatening to one's political career or contrary to one's political principles. A good case in
point is that of the UDN. When Quadros resigned,
the National Democratic Union, whose candidate he had
been, announced that it continued to support the
programs of structural reforms that had been called

for by the ex-president. Magalhães Pinto, governor
of the state of Minas Gerais and leader of the party
at the time, declared in October 1961 that if land
reform and other structural and social reforms were
delayed, Brazil would find itself in danger of massive social upheaval.[11] He counseled the nation to
put into effect the reformist promises that Jânio
had made. Senator Milton Campos, who had presided
over the former president's Special Commission for
Agrarian Reform, introduced a moderate land reform
bill into the Senate in August 1961. The UDN apparently felt that so long as the reformist initiative
was in its own hands reformist policy would remain
nonthreatening. The party leadership therefore
fostered the Campos bill through the Senate to a
favorable vote at the end of 1962. In the meantime,
the party evidently felt safe enough behind the protection of the parliamentary system and the constitutional change which had put land taxation in the
hands of municípios, to publicly endorse President
Goulart's statement in favor of basic reforms in June
of the same year.[12]

Within a month of Congress' reconvening in March
of 1963, however, the UDN position changed radically.
Two divisive issues had arisen to provoke a fight within party ranks leading to the ultimate triumph of the
anti-reform faction. The first issue was that of the
president's insistence, by way of his prime minister's
speech to Congress in August 1962, that it was abso-
lutely necessary that the national legislature pass a
land reform law accompanied by an amendment to the
constitution changing the provisions affecting expropriation of land. An important segment of UDN opinion viewed such a proposition with discomfort, if not

135

alarm, and felt that the UDN should go on record as categorically opposed to any such constitutional change, especially now that Goulart was invested with full presidential powers. The second issue was one of party control and presidential aspiration. The UDN pro-reform position had been articulated by party leader Magalhães Pinto. Carlos Lacerda, governor of Guanabara, and the single most dedicated opponent of Vargas and all his allies and heirs (Goulart was one of the latter), was determined to wrest UDN control from Magalhães Pinto. The two issues converged at the UDN convention in Curitíba in the state of Paraná at the end of April 1963. Lacerda presented the UDN leadership with an ultimatum. Either the UDN would clearly oppose any land reform proposal that was accompanied by a constitutional amendment, or he would retire from politics. Apparently, the prospect of being abandoned by the powerful UDN founding father when elections were looming on the horizon was too frightening. Anti-reform feeling within the party triumphed and a surprisingly strong majority voted against sweeping structural reforms and for Lacerda.[13]

Not all udenistas agreed with the party decision. A small group of reformists within the UDN, who called themselves the "bossa nova," argued that social conditions dictated the need for sweeping reforms, including modification of the constitution, and that the UDN must come out clearly in support for such reforms or be left behind. Repudiating the Carta de Princípios (letter of principles) issued at Curitiba, the group publicly endorsed a strong pro-structural reform position, including land reform based on amendment.[14] The bossa nova, however, was a small splinter group, and could not hope to turn around the vast bulk of the party. Nevertheless, its failure to conform to the stated party position did act as a thorn in the side of the party leadership.[15]

The PSD also underwent a process of reassessment from 1961 to early 1963. Its position, however, differed from that of the UDN. There was no doubt about the latter's opposition role to the PTB oriented government in power. Nor could the UDN pretend to exercise political leadership in the Congress since it was not the majority party in either of the two houses. By contrast, the PSD was the majority party in the Chamber of Deputies. The utility of reaching an understanding with the executive was dictacted by this and other good reasons. Prominent among them was the party's pragmatic, accommodationist inclination, as exemplified by its practice of entering alliances with the other Vargas-founded party, PTB; its habit of being in power and willingness to subordinate principle to political gain;[16] and, finally, the eagerness of the PSD leadership to take advantage of the populist payoff on the land reform issue. As a result, party head Amaral Peixoto (Vargas' son-in-law) announced in a formal statement from Brasília that the PSD was solidly behind reforms in general both because they were just and because they would act to control any revolutionary stirrings in the countryside. The PSD would urge its membership in the Congress to take positive action on two agrarian proposals that had been submitted by PSD deputies Gileno de Carli and José Joffily.[17] Ex-President Juscelino Kubitschek, who was already campaigning for his second presidential term, warned that it would be an "unspeakable crime" not to effect imme-

diately a sweeping reform program which would even
include a provision for enfranchising illiterate
people.[18]

The bandwagon approach to dealing with the administration's proposals generated opposition within
PSD ranks. The tension mounted between its essentially conservative landowning constituency, and the
party's leadership over the latter's desire for electoral reasons to keep apace of reformist policies of
the government. This caused the PSD to engage in the
never ending pursuit of an ideal compromise. By
April 1962, the necessity to come to terms with its
staunchly conservative and powerful faction from
Minas Gerais caused the PSD to modify its reformist
posture to the point that the Carta de Brasília (letter of Brasilia) which it produced that month strongly resembled the Carta de Princípios drafted by the
UDN under Lacerda's direction. Its former five-point
program on land reform, which had taken a favorable
stand on the issue of constitutional reform, was
pared down to a single vague sentence.[22] Amaral
Peixoto justified these changes in the PSD position
by arguing that, in fact, the party still supported
land reform and the amendment proposal, but that it
was pointless to make broad commitments without reference to specific legislation. After all, not all
land reform bills called for expropriation of land
payable in bonds.[20] By no means was this to be the
pessedista's final statement on the issue.

The third major party, the Brazilian Labor Party
(PTB), conformed to the strategy defined by its major
leader, President João Goulart. It was already clear
in 1962, however, that the radical wing of the party
under Brizola's leadership was gaining strength and

138

might be expected to behave less than docily towards the president's political scheming the following year.

The jockeying of the parties in Congress generated no conclusive results in 1962. Everyone, the president included, wished at that point to appear strongly and seriously pro-land reform without necessarily doing anything about it. Jango's Basic Reforms proposal was discussed alongside of other measures introduced by deputies and senators, but no major decisions were made. The president of the Chamber, Ranieri Mazilli, informed the prime minister in October that it was most unrealistic to expect any vote on agrarian reform that year. Too much else was on the agenda. In addition, the impending congressional elections were bound to absorb everyone's attention for what remained of that congressional session.[21] One deputy observed cryptically that the intensity and frequency of the inconclusive discussions on land reform were related directly to the election campaign, as could be seen from the precipitous drop in interest in the issue immediately after the elction.[22] It was not an entirely unproductive year in terms of rural benefits, however. For one thing, Congress approved the creation of SUPRA (Superintendency for Agrarian Reform). For another, the Chamber had approved, and sent to the Senate, the bill for the Rural Worker Statute calculated to extend to rural workers the rights and protection enjoyed by urban workers since the Vargas period. Finally, the Senate passed the Milton Campos bill and forwarded it to the Chamber.

Phase II: The Politics of Conciliation: Frustration and Disillusionment

Negotiation. When Congress reconvened in March 1963, the lines of battle were fairly clearly drawn. As anticipated, the presidential message to Congress, which presented the Three Year Plan drawn up by Celso Furtado as part of Goulart's positive left experiment, contained a strong statement on the urgent need for a large scale land reform. Such a reform program, the president insisted in his message, must be based on an easing of the constitutional provisions regarding expropriation and payment for land. The text of the amendment proposal offered by the president stipulated that expropriated land could be paid for in bonds redeemable in several payments over twenty years, with an interest of six percent, and liable to a maximum indexation for inflation of ten percent per year. The proposal also provided for the forced leasing of unused or underutilized land. The land reform bill Goulart presented to accompany the amendment proposal, which would be formally introduced to the Chamber by the PTB, stated that the purpose of the reform was to provide rural laborers with access to land to provide all with "the material and social conditions for a dignified life."[23]

Congressional party maneuvering from this point on would revolve around the issue of the presidential proposal. A special Chamber commission on land reform was created at the end of April in order to consider Goulart's agrarian legislation. The commission was to be composed of three deputies each from the PSD, the UDN, and the PTB, and one deputy each from the Social Progressive Party (a right wing party and personal vehicle of Adhemar de Barros) and the middle of the road Christian Democratic Party.[24] Thus, despite the fact that the Milton Campos bill had been introduced into the Chamber on April 5, that is, before Goulart's proposal, the president's measures would be the focus of interest from then on.

President Goulart and the PTB were determined to have the proposed amendment and law approved in an "extraordinary" single session by a two-thirds majority vote. It was hoped that enough pressure and momentum could be built up to actually get the measures ratified. The alternative was a longer process in which, during two separate sessions separated by a year, the measure was required to secure a majority vote in both houses. The PTB and its allies among the smaller parties feared that if the second procedure were used, the proposals would never be approved. There was still another alternative lurking in the wings, that of a plebiscite, as urged earlier by Prime Minister Tancredo Neves, and retired General Henrique Teixeira Lott.[25] Visão excitedly speculated that such a plebiscite could bring on a revolution, and "decree the failure of Brazilian representative democracy, which would then be ripe to welcome a Brazilian de Gaulle."[26] But this option never got beyond the speculation stage.

To secure the necessary number of votes for Goulart's objective, the PTB knew it would have to find support from among the members of the two other parties. Yet it was entirely out of the question that the UDN, with the exception of the small bossa nova wing, could be swayed in any way. It was also clear that there was no way of assuring the success for the negotiations with the majority party, PSD, in view of the fact that the deputies from Minas Gerais also seemed unmovable. The specific provisions of the PTB proposal did not in any way improve the chances for a compromise. Any constitutional change altering provisions on expropriation were bound to be considered a menace by conservatives and even moderates. The ten percent per year ceiling on the correction of bonds for inflation at a time when the prevailing rate of inflation was already eight times that made the measure totally unpalatable. Still, as the PTB perceived the state of affairs, the PSD was the only hope for passing the desired legislation.

The government was not entirely wrong in placing its hopes on the PSD. In spite of the conservative retreat it had tactically made at the end of 1962, the PSD leadership was always ready to consider any compromise that would enhance its lines of access to official power. The mineiro contingent was not about to change its mind about land reform, but the pessedista leadership decided that it had nothing to lose by negotiating with the Goulart government. Indeed, the Special Commission on Agrarian Reform had barely been formed when Gustavo Capanema, a prominent PSD affiliated jurist, began intensive work on a possible substitute to the PTB amendment.[27] Totaling up the possible votes for a suitably modified amendment, the PSD optimistically estimated the party vote in favor of an amendment would be as follows: PSD - 90 (firm) votes and perhaps another 20; UDN - 60; PTB - 20; PDC - 10; other parties - 20. This meant a total of 220 votes, or 52 short of the necessary minimum of 272.

Speculations on the breakdown of votes on land reform was entirely premature at this point. Even

while Amaral Peixoto was estimating the vote, the
mineiro deputies produced a public declaration stat-
ing that under no circumstances would they ever agree
to any kind of amendment affecting expropriation of
land.[28] While the PSD leadership turned its attention again to putting its house in order, the Special
Commission on Agrarian Reform presented its findings
on April 14. The Christian Democratic Party had been
asked to report on the draft of the amendment for the
commission, and it had issued a favorable statement.
The Commission as a whole, however, clearly disagreed
with PDC sentiments and rejected the recommendations
in a seven to four vote.

At this point, the discouraged Goulart made a
perfunctory attempt to meet with the party leaders of
the Chamber.[29] A meeting of this type might have
served a purpose before the special commission had
presented its report. Coming as late as it did after
the commission vote defeating the presidential proposal, the meeting served only to reinforce Goulart's
frustration and contributed to his decision to abandon the serious programs and objectives of the positive left. He sullenly removed himself from the congressional discussion, at least for the time being.
The immediate effect of his abrupt withdrawal was
that the leadership of the left on land reform fell
to Brizola. He, in turn, was perceived as enough of
a threat to stimulate further mobilization of the
anti-reformist forces, thereby polarizing the situation even more.[30]

No one was happy with the situation. UDN deputy Saldanha Derzi articulated the suspicions of the
opposition that the reformist campaign was deliberately manipulated and politicized, and not a reflec-

143

tion of genuine rural needs. He noted that it was strange that the pressure for land reform was coming "from the General Workers' Command, from railroad workers, from dock workers, from sergeants, from bank workers, but not from those most concerned: the farmer."[31] The conservatives feared the worst was yet to come. The PTB and its allies were defeated for the moment and not encouraged by future prospects. Those who sympathized with the reformist aims and attempted to find a way of supporting the administration were, to say the least, frustrated.

In an editorial titled "7 x 4" (referring to the breakdown of votes in the Special Commission on Agrarian Reform) the Correio da Manhã addressed the urgent need for reforms in Brazil:

> But what happens? The most urgent demands of the country are introduced by a party of /PTB/ pelegos and rejected by the coroneis of the PSD, now reinforced, shamefully, by the coroneis and bachareis of the UDN. . . . This two-sided demogoguery prospers because of the lack of true national leadership. . . .[32]

A member of the bossa nova of the UDN, Deputy Edison Garcia from Mato Grosso, was more explicit in his accusations, which were aimed primarily at the president himself.

> At this time, when the possibility seems remote that the National Congress will give the country an agrarian reform based on constitutional reform, it behooves us. . . to point out the responsibility of the . . . Federal Government itself, in the person of Sr. João Goulart. . . . If it be true that the /President/ truly wants to give the country a reform, that fact is belied by the composition of his cabinet, by the obligations he assumes to men committed to the present economic and political structure of the country. . . . A government. . . that feasts with those it accuses of being exploiters of the people. . . /needs/ to begin by serving as a

144

better example.[33]

For the president and the PTB, the negative report of the special commission was but the first round
in its battles with the opposition in the Chamber.
The next step would be to bring the amendment proposal, along with the negative committee report to a vote
in a plenary session of Congress. The PTB was well
aware of the fact that at this point, given the climate that prevailed in the Chamber, the proposal would
no doubt suffer a resounding defeat. Stalling for
time, the PTB therefore employed obstructionist tactics to prevent an immediate discussion of the amendment.

The PSD saw in this situation an opportunity to
act as mediator and conciliator, thereby ingratiating
itself with the government. Following directly on the
heels of the report of the special commission, and
ignoring the grumbling of the mineiro contingent, the
PSD leadership produced its own proposal for an amendment. The measure was offered in an obvious spirit of
pragmatic compromise. The PSD was willing to accommodate itself to the PTB position by supporting the
idea of constitutional reform of those provisions affecting expropriation, and by agreeing to the principle of payment in bonds. In return, however, it insisted on a redefinition of the specific expropria-
tionist provisions of the amendment. Expropriations
could be made only of unproductive properties that
were over 500 hectares (1,235.5 acres); correction for
inflation of bonds would be raised to fifty percent
(from Goulart's ten percent); expropriations could be
made only in areas designated as part of regional
plans approved by Congress; only the federal govern-

ment would have the authority to expropriate land; and, finally, the Senate would have the authority to confirm the nominations to the organization established to conduct the reform.[34]

As might be expected, an official proposal to alter constitutional provisions regarding land expropriation made by the "party of fazendeiros" (landowners) itself was greeted by reactions ranging from disbelief, to apathy, to delight. UDN Deputy Francelino Pereira (from Minas Gerais) dismissed the PSD proposal as a PTB amendment in sheep's clothing.[35] Deputy Plínio Sampaio, a Christian Democrat who worked particularly hard for an amendment, observed sardonically that the PSD was finally getting in touch with national reality--whereupon pessedista Peracchi Barcelos (from Rio Grande do Sul) took strong exception to the statement, declaring to his "noble colleague, that the PSD has always been integrated into Brazilian reality."[36] A Visão editorial exulted that:

> We are. . . faced with an almost accomplished fact:
> that of the approval by Congress this year, within
> a period of three months, of an agrarian reform.
> This approval would signify a victory of reform
> over revolution, that is, of reform understood as
> it should be: anti-revolution.[37]

Not everyone shared this happy view of the situation. The president remained withdrawn and silent. The PTB however, had no reservations about expressing its displeasure with the PSD proposal. It pronounced the PSD proposal a pretext for setting up a thriving real estate business, and a sell-out of the principle of land reform which, the PTB felt, should put the burden of the cost on the landowners themselves, who were responsible for social and economic exploitation in the countryside.

The first half of the second phase of the agrarian policy debate thus ended on a discordant note of disillusionment and incipient radicalization. The president's program of "responsible reforms" had not met with the enthusiasm he looked for on the part of the moderates, and had drawn the criticism of radicals growing impatient with the administration's failure to produce reforms both in policy and in practice. Goulart's reaction to the situation was to abandon the "positive left" and give himself up to the politics of populist radicalism.

Jango's renunciation of the positive reform approach did not in any sense mean that he was rid of the necessity of dealing with Congress. So long as he was operating within the rules of the game, and especially because of the narrowness of his support among established elites, the Congress would continue to be the source of any and all reformist measures he wished to see passed. Consequently, Goulart's credibility with his own labor constituency had to be based not only on a radicalization of his rhetoric and on his support for strikes and demonstrations, but also on his ability to convert some of his reformist promises into law. In this, he had to depend on, and therefore negotiate with Congress.

Frustration. The necessity of doing so was brought home with particular force not only for Goulart, but also for the PTB membership in the third week of June 1963, marking an alteration in the tenor of the congressional debate. The UDN, appalled at the radicalization of the country, and uneasy over the PSD's apparent willingness to at least entertain the idea of a constitutional amendment, decided to make doubly sure that the PTB amendment proposal would be defeated at

147

whatever point it was brought to a vote. The UDN
strategy centered on a revival of the Milton Campos
bill, which, following its approval by the Senate, had
been shelved by the Chamber in order to deal immediately with the Goulart-PTB measures. On June 18,
despite PTB and PSD efforts to prevent a quorum by
urging their members to absent themselves, there were
enough deputies present to approve the UDN motion to
have the Campos bill reclassified "urgent" and therefore brought up for immediate consideration.[38] As a
result, despite any objections the PTB had to the
PSD amendment or reservations as to a possible partnership, the labor party put them in abeyance for the
time being. The time for the vote on the Campos bill
was fast approaching. Concerned that the bill might
stand a chance of passing unless the PSD declined to
support it, Goulart called in Mário Martins Rodrigues,
PSD leader in the Chamber, for a conference. The
president argued strongly for the necessity to enact
a land reform law accompanied by a constitutional
amendment. He noted with displeasure that the PSD
had helped reject an unfavorable report on the Campos
bill in the Economic Commission of the Chamber and
thereby had contributed to its chances of passage.
Rodrigues obligingly responded that the PSD was not
against a constitutional amendment, and would be most
happy to cooperate with the government provided, of
course, they could agree on an amendment more moderate than the Goulart-PTB draft.[39]

At this impasse, Goulart could have opted to allow the Campos bill to be considered immediately, and
even passed, since he could always veto it. However,
he was well aware that this would delay consideration
of his own measures by several months, and could

even pose the danger that Congress might override his veto. This was a risk Jango was not prepared to run. Within three day's time, Goulart and the PSD leadership in the Chamber had worked out a compromise formula, closely resembling the original PSD amendment proposal.[40]

Although the president and the PSD leadership had agreed on a formula, the success of the new partnership and its ability to defeat the Campos bill depended on the approval of both the mineiro wing of the PSD and of the general membership of the PTB in the Chamber. The former evidently was less of a problem than the latter. The PSD deputies granted approval to the formula within two days of the presidential agreement with the PSD. The PTB, however, was not so docile, and its radical faction was reluctant to offer even formal support regardless of the immediate advantages. The PSD, determined to preserve the terms of the bargain, made it clear that unless the PTB supported the compromise, it would not guarantee that its deputies would vote against the Campos bill.

The month of July was given over to finding a way of reconciling the competing interests and ideologies of the PTB and the PSD while avoiding a definitive vote on the Campos bill. The Estado de São Paulo, one of Brazil's most prestigious newspapers, expressed incomprehension over the failure by opponents of the Campos bill to act, since they could have contributed to a quorum with their presence.[41] The deputies were, of course, aware of this. But the PSD wished to avoid a vote on the bill until the PTB committed itself to supporting the pessedista amendment proposal. Once the votes were taken, the PTB might

149

no longer be in nearly so conciliatory a mood. In
the two week period from July 24 to August 7 the
Campos bill was brought up for a vote seven times,
without its backers being able to raise a quorum. To
break the impasse, the PSD was forced to decide whether it would take the word of Goulart and of his supporting faction in the PTB as a sign of formal agreement on the compromise proposal, or, more realistically withhold its support until, and unless the radical ideological wing of the PTB, the compactos,
agreed to the measure as well. Ultimately, the PSD
desire to accommodate itself to the situation and get
the vote over with before the mineiros again became
unmanageable prevailed. As a result, the Campos bill
was finally voted on in a quorum on August 7, 1963.
The votes were 69 for, and 164 against, with two ab-
stentions. The Campos bill was formally dead.[42]

To a group of deputies from several parties who
had watched this strategic play evolve and fail, it
seemed self evident that any proposals originating
with the PTB or the UDN were bound to go down in defeat, not because of the intrinsic qualities of the
measures, but because neither party would vote for
any bill introduced by the other. Some way had to be
found out of this impasse, if only to be able to go
on to other congressional business. Accordingly,
even before the final vote was taken on the Campos
bill, a new solution was being considered to the
agrarian legislative impasse. A prominent UDN politician approached Deputy Aniz Badra, a Christian
Democrat from São Paulo, and pointed out that the
Campos bill had passed the Senate, and would have
also passed the Chamber, if it were not for the strict-
ly political issue of sponsorship.[43] If a similar

bill were to be introduced by a deputy from a "neutral" party, the chances that it would be approved in the Chamber with most parties supporting it, including a portion of the PTB, were very good.

Within eight days Badra had patched together a what appeared a modified version of the Campos bill, and obtained the necessary number of signatures to have it put on the calendar of the Chamber. As anticipated, even the Goulart faction of the PTB was persuaded to lend its support by the argument that this was the only way out of the impasse, and that the PTB amendment would still be considered, albeit separately. Also, support for scheduling the bill did not imply an obligation on the part of the PTB to vote for it later. The Badra bill was officially introduced on August 6, one day beforethe Campos bill was defeated, as anticipated.

Exhausted by the frenzied activity around the agrarian issue, the leaders of the PSD majority, Tancredo Nêves, and the UDN minority, Pedro Aleixo, proposed that the debate on the PTB-Goulart amendment be postponed for ten sessions. The suggestion was readily approved. The month of August was a dead month in terms of the agrarian issue. Even newspapers reduced their intensive coverage of agrarian unrest to a mere few articles. The PTB-PSD discussions on the compromise amendment degenerated into a parlay on appointments and agreements by which the PSD might be induced to change the constitutional provisions on land reform.[44]

These doldrums, and the desultory negotiations between the PSD and the PTB dragged to an end by the end of August, when the PTB leader in the Chamber, Bocayuva Cunha, announced on the 29th of August that it was time to resume the discussion of the amendment and stop shirking the "historic responsibility" that the deputies were facing.[45] The PTB had clearly come to a final determination as to what to do about the amendment and the discussions with the PSD. The compactos -- i.e., the ideologues -- had prevailed within the party, with the result that the Goulart-PTB compromise was rejected in preference to the original version of the amendment drafted by the PTB. If there had been any doubt before, it was clear now that the alliance with the PSD forged on the eve of the vote for the Campos bill had been very ultilitarian indeed.

The discussion of the Goulart-PTB amendment was to be the final important encounter between the sponsors of the measure and the opposition. However, little effort or interest on the part of the government actually went into this last contest in the politics of conciliation. The president remained aloof and uninvolved in what he doubtlessly considered an inevitable defeat, thus contributing to the hopelessness of the situation. Considering the importance of both the occasion and the issue, the discussion of the amendment began most inauspiciously on September 6. Out of a total of 409 deputies, only 40 were present. Of these 40, only four were members of the PTB. The labor party clearly considered the defeat of the amendment to be a foregone conclusion. As the Correio da Manhã commented, "The other one hundred five deputies of the PTB were notable only by their absence."[46]

The discussion of the next month, prior to a final vote on the Goulart amendment, consisted of a reiteration of by now familiar political positions.

After several unsuccessful attempts, a quorum was
finally secured on October seventh. A total of 72
votes were needed to approve the amendment.[47] In an
atmosphere of depression and disillusionment, the
amendment went down in defeat, with 121 votes for,
and 176 against it. As if to emphasize that this was
the end of an era, the government promptly dismissed
Deputy Bocayuva Cunha as PTB leader in the Chamber.
For the PSD, this action constituted final proof of
the absence of any serious commitment on the government's part to find a solution to the legislative
impasse. The tenuous PSD -- government alliance was
at an end.

Phase III: The Politics of Disintegration

The defeat of the amendment signified the end of
legislative discussion of land reform. It also marked the end of political dialogue and conciliation as
a government strategy to attain its reformist objectives. Signaling the onset of a new politics of confrontation, the president requested decree powers
from Congress in October 1963. Recognizing the fu-
tility of the request, which recalled the crisis precipitated one year earlier by Jânio Quadros, Goulart
quickly withdrew the proposal.

Congress was clearly relieved. There was no
possibility that it would have acceded to such a request (the military permitting) since it would have
enabled Jango to attain by other means what Congress
was unwilling to grant through ordinary legislation.
But discussion of decree powers would have constituted still another element of controversy in an
already impossible impasse.

Congressional relief over the elimination of

this additional source of strife was mitigated, however, by Goulart's total withdrawal from any further
political dialogue with Congress. This act left
Congress severely reduced in influence. So long as
the president dealt with the legislature, the latter
could exert some influence over the course of events.
His rebuff left Congress in the role of an anguished
and impotent spectator. At the close of the normal
session, it continued to sit in extraordinary session for the duration of the recess, while SUPRA, the
agrarian reform agency, became the new focus of
public attention.

Within Congress, all deliberation on pending
agrarian legislation was suspended while discussion
centered on the forthcoming SUPRA decree which would
give the president power to expropriate land along
roadways, dams, and wells. The PTB and small leftist parties absented themselves entirely from these
discussions, while PSD and UND representatives monopolized the floor, calling unsuccessfully for the
abolition of SUPRA.

In forsaking his congressional strategy, Goulart
made the decision to abandon any semblance of constitutional and conciliatory behavior. His only alternative avenue of influence lay in mobilizing mass
support for his radical policies and bringing it to
bear on the conservative opposition both within Congress and the nation as a whole. In other words,
Goulart's strategy shifted from accommodation and
conciliation within the political system to a policy
of confrontation about it. Unfortunately for Jango,
he raised the stakes of the conflict without ade-
quate power to prevail against the corporate elite.
Radical demonstrations succeeded in shaking but not

154

intimidating conservative forces. Ironically, once
Goulart opened the contest to extra-constitutional
means of resolving the existing impasse, he virtually set into motion predictable patterns of corporatist mobilization and repulsion. Thus, his radical populist measures succeeded not in bringing about
needed structural reforms in Brazil, but in paving
the way for military takeover and the return to authoritarian rule.

THE CONGRESS AND CASTELO

Congressional discussion of land reform under
Castelo Branco was strikingly different from what had
gone on under Goulart. For reasons examined earlier,
the nature of executive-congressional relations had
rather dramatically changed, giving the executive an
advantage even in the treatment of an issue potentially as redistributive as land reform. The actual
amount of time Congress had for the discussion of the
land reform law and constitutional amendment introduced by the president was severely limited. This
was only in small part due to the purge of leftist
representatives. Congress had its agenda full of
important issues generated by the revolution. More
important, however, once the measures themselves were
submitted in October 1964, the Congress had only
thirty days in which to decide what it was going to
do with them. Otherwise, it risked witnessing their
automatic passage into law, unaltered, at the end of
that period. The overall character of the legislative debate on land reform under Castelo was thus
quite different since actual discussion of the proposals, even during the time they were up for consideration was much more circumscribed than pre-

viously. The legislative constraint and the censorship imposed by the new regime were reflected in the
fact that newspaper coverage of land reform, which
before had been intensive, was now practically nonexistent. As much as it was an issue of foremost
public concern before the revolution, agrarian reform seemed to be an internal matter to be settled
between the president and the politicians in Congress who had contributed to the success of the revolution. To be sure, the privatized atmosphere of
the discussions was in no small part due to the fact
that an important sector of the political public
which existed at the time of Goulart was now purged,
its political rights abolished, many of its leaders
exiled or in prison, and its membership placed under
strict observation and control. This was true of the
radical political leadership, the urban workers, and
perhaps most importantly, for the fledgling rural
organizations, which perished under the blow of the
revolution.

Within Congress, the mood among deputies supporting the revolution was somewhat somber, but re-
laxed. The purge of the populist part of the political spectrum left the Congress provisionally in the
hands of the UDN and a good part of the PSD. The UDN
now became the government party, and basked in the
knowledge that "its" president was again in office to
pick up, perhaps, where the hapless Jânio Quadros had
left off. The expansiveness of the atmosphere
prompted suggestions by some deputies that those involved in agricultural disturbances (promoting land
invasions, demonstrations, squatting), be given an
amnesty.[48] The Badra bill, which had been introduced
into the Chamber on an urgent note and debated off

and on while the Goulart-PTB amendment was being discussed and even during the first week after the revolution, seemed to have been forgotten in the general relief of the conservatives felt over the disappearance of Goulart.

The sense of relief the conservatives were experiencing in regard to what they thought would be the demise of the agrarian issue, at least on the terms that Goulart had posed it (i.e., constitutional amendment), was to be short lived, however. By the end of May there could be no dout that Castelo was quite serious in his intention to have articles 141 and 146 of the constitution amended and a land reform law passed. In point of fact, Minister of Planning Roberto Campos was already hard at work on the matter. The revolution's allies in Congress suddenly found themselves faced with the prospect of opposing their government on the very issue that had contributed so materially to their supporting the military's ouster of Jango. From the Congress, Deputy Ivan Luz appealed to Castelo: "President! Free the Revolution at any price from the infantile illness of reformism, which was so much to the taste of the adolescents of a very recent past."[49] Such appeals apparently fell on deaf ears, since even UDN leader João Mendes seemed to be unable to influence the government. An attempt to renew interest in the Badra bill as a means forestalling government policy resulted in Chamber approval of the measure in August. This maneuver in no way influenced the president's determination to secure the passage of his own measures. The consultations the president called between the land reform task force and congressional leaders seemed to be more for the purpose of informing the

157

leaders of the president's intentions than of actually soliciting congressional opinion. The UDN, victim
of revolutionary irony, again found itself in the
role of principal opposition. Notwithstanding its
anxiety to see the measure defeated and also to find
some means of resolving the differences with "its"
government, the UDN leadership could not come up with
the heralded viable alternative to the presidential
measures.

The _castelista_ proposals were presented to Congress in a joint session on October 21. The UDN was
ready for the encounter with over 400 amendments
which would, as Deputy Cid Carvalho said, change
ninety-five percent of the proposal. The major issue
now was whether and how the UDN could be made to
change its position. To all appearances, the old
lines of battle were redrawn. The UDN was the source
of opposition to the measures, the PTB was arguing in
their favor (although this was no longer its government, but rather, one to which it was supposedly opposed) and the PSD, as ever, was anxious to please
the government in power and follow the path of least
resistance. Deputy Último de Carvalho, a landowner
from Minas Gerais, member of the PSD and the congressman with the singular distinction of having made
more speeches on land reform during the period under
consideration than anyone else,expressed his disillusionment and chagrin with revolutionary policy thus:

> It is an irony of fate that the sponsors are the
> same, the very same ones, who one year ago were
> responsible for the political nuptials of the ex-
> president with the communists by means of constitu-
> tional amendment No.1 of 1963. The legislative of-
> ficers are the same; the procedure -- the same; the
> mained constitutional principle -- the same; the
> amendment, in its essence -- the same, the one

> differing from the other merely in the identity
> of the /presidential/ signatories. He of the João
> Goulart amendment /is in/ bitter exile; he of the
> Castelo Branco amendment is President of the
> Republic.50

The situation was not entirely identical, however, to the extent that the UDN was now the majority party and therefore controlled the Chamber commissions. Of equal importance was the fact that the government was determined that all accommodations be arrived at in private consultation and not by means of congressional discussion.

The deadlock in the agrarian commission was finally broken when udenista Pacheco Chaves resigned as reporter on the bill for the commission and was replaced by Brazilian Socialist Party Deputy Aurélio Vianna who favored land reform and could be trusted to produce a favorable report. But the most important undertaking was to neutralize UDN opposition by prevailing on the party leadership to do away with party discipline to allow its members to vote as they wished.[51] Following intensive last-minute sessions with the president, majority leader João Mendes agreed.

With an overwhelming vote, the government thus got its constitutional amendment and Land Statute, making possible a land reform based on expropriation payable in bonds. This provision was the government's single most important victory. On other points it made the concessions and compromises which made possible the amendment and Land Statute in the first place. An accompanying amendment which would have established a separate court system for rural justice was defeated. Compensation for land would be in bonds, but any other, man-made properties on the

159

land, i.e., buildings, roads, wells, machinery, etc., would have to be paid for in cash. Bonds would be redeemable at a value reflecting full correction for inflation. Finally, the government was only partially successful in attempting to reverse the 1961 amendment which gave municípios the right to collect land taxes. The federal government would set the tax rates, but it would have to give most of the proceeds to state and município governments for redistribution.

Deputy Último de Carvalho, whose bitter musings are quoted above, vacillated between despair over the possibility that Brazil was seeing the last days of private property, and the somewhat brighter thought that, as he put it, "engagement is not marriage." Between the passage of a law and the application of it much could happen. For perhaps the first time he found himself in agreement with some PTB deputies who expressed serious doubts that the government would actually carry out a land reform.

In the final analysis, the measures passed were a compromise, but one in which the government enjoyed the greater victory. For in spite of the concessions, the amendment and statute created the mechanisms making land reform possible. From this point on it would be possible for the government to expropriate property and pay for it in bonds rather than in cash. The power of expropriation, together with an agrarian law establishing institutes of agrarian reform and development constituted the basis for a broad and potentially effective policy of rural development and social change. Ultimately, however, the opinion of the conservatives that the saving grace of the measures would be the improbability of their implementation turned out to be correct.

Notwithstanding the charges of betrayal that the hard core anti-reformists leveled against the administration, they had little to fear. The Castelo land reform law was a political aberration, inconsistent with the policy course which would be followed by succeeding administrations. It was the direct result of the president's concern with rural unrest and his personal determination to grant a symbolic concession to the restive masses on whom the revolution's economic policies would weigh most heavily. Future administrations, armed with stronger decree powers, would exhibit less delicacy in considering the sensibilities of the masses.

The land reform experience was a showcase of congressional immobilism and inefficacy. As an institution, Congress was as much contributor to as victim of the crisis which ushered in an authoritarian regime. Caught in a fundamental contradiction, elected officials courted new constituencies through populist appeals while circumventing most serious attempts to deliver on reformist promises for fear of jeopardizing their immediate interests. There remains some doubt as to the seriousness of Congress' intent to participate in a fundamental transformation of the social system implied by land reform, or its ability, for that matter, to effect such reform in the face of concerted corporatist resistance. Contented to accommodate to strategies of ideological inconsistency and political opportunism, in the final analysis, they were Goulart's unthinking allies in the destruction of populist democracy.

NOTES

1. ICOPS, p.43.

2. Schmitter, p.258, Leff, pp.149-150, no. 29. Both Schmitter and Leff point out that the legislature is not generally the focus of interest group activity.

3. Eloy Dutra, IBAD, Sigla da Corrupção (Rio de Janeiro: Civilização Brasileira, 1963), p.

4. Visão, November 9, 1962, p. 12.

5. Ibid., p. 11.

6. The IPES files, for instance, contain the notation that an expenditure of $Cr. 300,000,000 was being planned to support fifteen "approved" candidates for national deputy. IPES. Executive Committee Meeting, May 15, 1962.

7. October 7, 1960, p. 15.

9. JB, January 3, 1961, p.3.

10. Dep. Aderbal Jurema, PSD, Pernambuco, JB, March 27, 1962, p.4.

11. JB, October 3, 1961, p. 11.

12. JB, June 21, 1962, p. 1.

13. Cf., JB and CM, April 21 to April 30, 1963.

14. CM, June 4, 1964, p. 10.

15. The following incident serves as an example: UDN member Oscar Correa criticized bossa nova member José Aparecido for embracing Brizola following a speech by the latter against the government's purchase of foreign companies, instead of direct nationalization. Aparecido replied that since he could not embrace the speech, with which he agreed, he embraced its author. CM, June 1, 1963, 10.

16. It had always been the majority party since 1945, and until 1961 when udenista Jânio Quadros took office, all post World War II presidents were pessedistas.

17. JB, August 25, 1961, p. 3.

18. Ibid., 28.1.1962, p.1.

162

19. <u>JB</u>, April 4, 1962, p.3.

20. Ibid., April 5, 1962, p. 3.

21. <u>JB</u>, May 10, 1962, p. 3.

22. Dep. Valério Magalhães, PSD, Rondônia, <u>Anais</u>, XXI, 1962, 174 ses., Nov. 12.

23. Camara dos Deputados, reprint of amendment and bill, p.1.

24. <u>CM</u>, April 23, 1963, p.6.

25. Lott who was among the generals demanding Vargas' resignation in 1954, served as War Minister in 1955.

26. May 17, 1963, p. 11.

27. <u>CM</u>, April 28, 1963, p. 6.

28. Ibid., May 11, 1963, p. 6.

29. Ibid., May 15, 1963.

30. <u>Visão</u>, May 24, 1963, p. 11.

31. <u>Anais</u>, VI 1968, 40 ses. May 15, p. 742.

32. May 15, 1963, p. 6.

33. IBID., VI 1963, 40 ses. May 15, pp. 690-691.

34. Ibid., Vol. VII, 1963, 48 ses., May 24, pp. 673-674. Report of Clovis Pestana, PSD-Minas Gerais defining PSD position on agrarian reform. See also <u>Visão</u>, May 31, 1963, p. 11.

35. Anais, Vol. XI 1963, 110 ses. July 23, pp. 379-380.

36. Ibid., Vol. VII, 1963, 49 ses. May 27, pp. 867-868.

37. May 31, 1963, p. 11.

38. <u>CM</u>, June 19, 1963, p. 14.

39. Ibid., July 7, 1963, p. 13.

40. The yearly correction for inflation would be to the extent of fifty percent; property that might be subject to expropriation had to cover an area of at least 500 hectares and be located at least fifty kilometers outside of cities of a

population of 50,000 or more. Also, regardless of what the total land area might be, land of which at least fifty percent was in use could not be expropriated. <u>Correio da Manhã</u>, 10.7. 1963, p.8, 1-2.

41. July 12, 1963, also July 26, 1963.

42. <u>Anais</u>, Vol. XVII 1963, 124 ses. August 7, p.181.

43. The politician in question was either Aleixo or Rondon Pacheco, according to information secured in interviews.

44. <u>CM</u>, August 1, 1963, p.12.

45. <u>Anais</u>, XIX 1963, 142 ses., August 29, p.573.

46. September 7, 1963, p.12.

47. <u>Anais</u>, Vol. XXVI, 1963, ses. 198, Oct. 7, pp.225-240.

48. Ibid., Vol. II, 1964, ses. 10, March 30. Waldmar Alves, PST--Pernambuco.

49. Ibid., Vol. XI, 1964, 86 ses., June 16, p.442.

50. Ibid., XXVII 1964, 204 ses., Oct. p.155.

51. This unique behavior on the part of the UDN was the product of its special relationship with the government, encouraging it to view itself as privileged, and also of the deliberate pains the president took to respect a certain degree of congressional autonomy.

5. Political Behavior and the Land Reform Debate

The institutional perspective of the preceding chapter provided a means of assessing the impact of congressional behavior on the definition and eventual resolution of issues. The observed aggregate response of the Brazilian Congress to the land reform issue consisted predominantly of a myopic preoccupation with immediate political gain modified by secondary ideological and programmatic concerns. The political strategies pursued by parties and factions with the president fixed on securing new constituencies with which to buttress existing power bases. Consequently, the exploitation of fashionable reformist issues like land reform, while appearing politically advantageous, ultimately undermined the stability of Brazilian democracy and of the Congress itself.

This chapter compliments the foregoing discussion with a closer examination of the attitudes and legislative record of the deputies in the Chamber. An analysis of the agrarian debates provides a more detailed view of what the legislators perceived to be the true political implications of the land reform issue, what they felt were the appropriate strategies under the circumstances, and how they justified their attitudes and votes.

The ensuing examination of political attitudes

is based on a content analysis of the debates on land reform in the Chamber of Deputies from 1962 to the passage of the Land Statute in May 1964. The sample consists of the one hundred eighty-six deputies who participated in the agrarian debates at any point in this twenty-nine month period.[1]

The discussion is divided into two sections. The first explores the extent to which particular attitudes on land reform are associated with the geographic origin of deputies. In other words, an attempt is made to define a deputy's propensity to support structural reforms in terms of the level of economic development of his state of origin, and particularly of its agricultural sector. The second section examines the relevance of party identification to intensity of interest and to attitudes. Besides indicating a possible propensity of certain parties for populist issues, it explores the degree to which particular parties were influenced by short-term pragmatic considerations of access to clientelistic resources enabling them to extend their power base.

REGIONAL AND ECONOMIC INFLUENCES ON LEGISLATIVE BEHAVIOR

During the periods of its existence and active participation in the governmental process, the Brazilian Congress has served as a major arena for the expression of regional interests. This regionalism has reflected the extraordinary diversity -- economic, geographic, and social -- contained within the national borders. To a considerable degree, the extent of regional power and even of representation in the legislature have been influenced by the strength and importance of regional economies. Thus, during the

166

Old Republic, the constitutional establishment of a
federal government of equal states was mitigated by
the domination of São Paulo and Minas Gerais over
other states and the control this "coffee and milk"
agreement exercised over the presidency.

The unequal access of all areas of Brazil to
power has also been exacerbated by a bias in the
electoral process toward rural states and to rural
areas within states. The "politics of the governors"
may have ended officially with the revolution of
1930, but the continued survival of the coroneis and
of the state political machines was clearly evident
after the reestablishment of electoral politics
following World War II.

Since Congress enjoyed a relatively great degree of influence in the political arena during the
agrarian reform debates, the legislative discussions
should provide some idea of the range of regional
attitudes and intensity of interest on the part of
the various states in the issue. To measure intensity two indicators were used in the analysis. One
consisted of noting what percent of a particular
state's delegation participated in the debate at all.
The second consisted of recording repeated participation in the debates by state representatives already
identified as participants in the first case. The
intensity of interest was then related to the general economic and demographic characteristics of that
state. This procedure permits some assessment of
whether the primary reason for a high degree of interest in the land reform issue is related to specific economic conditions, to political considerations, or both.

In view of the fact that the land reform debate

was allegedly generated by acute social and economic
problems in depressed rural areas, we might reasonably expect that these areas, such as the Northeast,
would be most prominently represented in the debates.
Such an expectation is reinforced by the rural bias
of congressional representation. In fact, however,
the pattern and frequency of participation appears
only tangentially related to rural depression and unrest. Figure 5-1, an overview of delegate participation by state, suggests that interest in land reform was greatest in the southern and eastern states.[2]
This finding is clearly reinforced by Figure 5-2,
which presents a regional view of Brazil. The regional demographic data indicate that the greatest
participation in the land reform debate was by deputies from those regions that are the most populous,
wealthiest, most urban, and have the largest electorate (literate persons over eighteen). For example, two of the most active state delegations were
those of Guanabara (97.5 percent urban) and São
Paulo (62.8 percent urban). It would thus appear
that a relatively high degree of urbanization, and
not necessarily the predominence of agriculture,
stimulated interest in land reform, at least among
politicians. A review of frequency of participation
by individual deputies also indicates that the most
interested representatives came from the most populous states, and from those with the largest electorates. The interest in land reform of delegations
from the depressed, agricultural, and impoverished
Northeast is outweighed by that of the South and
East, where agriculture remains an important part of
the economy (e.g., coffee export production in São
Paulo, livestock in Rio Grande do Sul) but is commer-

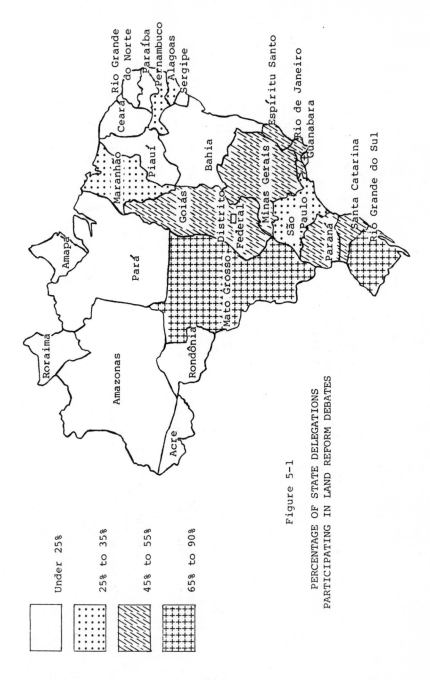

Figure 5-1

PERCENTAGE OF STATE DELEGATIONS
PARTICIPATING IN LAND REFORM DEBATES

Under 25%

25% to 35%

45% to 55%

65% to 90%

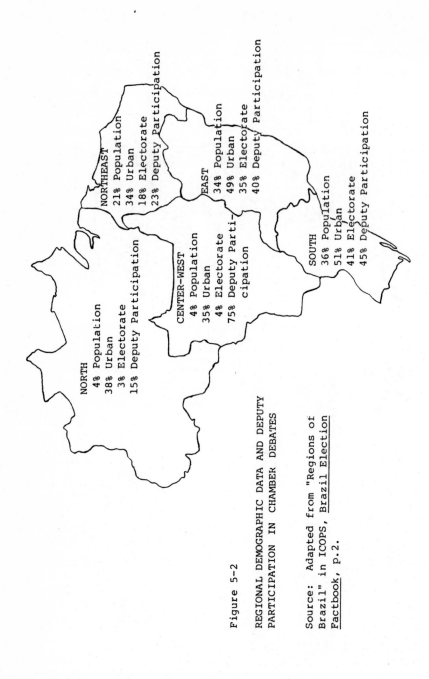

NORTH
4% Population
38% Urban
3% Electorate
15% Deputy Participation

NORTHEAST
21% Population
34% Urban
18% Electorate
23% Deputy Participation

CENTER-WEST
4% Population
35% Urban
4% Electorate
75% Deputy Parti-
cipation

EAST
34% Population
49% Urban
35% Electorate
40% Deputy Participation

SOUTH
36% Population
51% Urban
41% Electorate
45% Deputy Participation

Figure 5-2

REGIONAL DEMOGRAPHIC DATA AND DEPUTY
PARTICIPATION IN CHAMBER DEBATES

Source: Adapted from "Regions of
Brazil" in ICOPS, Brazil Election
Factbook, p.2.

cialized to some degree and complemented by relatively high industrial and urban growth. The keen interest of urban politicians in land reform might be explained by the prevalence of populist politics in their districts. Land reform, with its reformist implications, was an ideal populist issue.

In order to ascertain the accuracy of this inference, state delegations were reviewed for the intensity of their interest in the agrarian issue. Two criteria were used to indicate the states most involved in the land reform debate. One was that the state in question must have contributed at least ten percent of all speeches made on land reform; the other was that at least one member of the delegation have proposed at least one measure related to agriculture. Judged by these two criteria, Pernambuco, Minas Gerais, Rio de Janeiro, Guanabara, São Paulo, and Rio Grande do Sul demonstrated greatest involvement in the agrarian debate (table 5-1). All these states were in fact at least forty percent urban at the time, although the actual percentage of urbanization ranged from a low of forty percent in Minas Gerais to ninety-seven point five percent in Guanabara. Nevertheless, a closer scrutiny of the states' economies suggests that however significant, urbanization alone does not serve as a sufficient explanation. The states in question varied considerably in degrees of urbanization. Equally significant, they differed considerably in their levels of industrialization (with São Paulo heavily in the lead), and in the nature and organization of their agricultural production. It ranged from an emphasis on commercial agriculture (São Paulo), to small independent farming (Rio Grande do Sul), to traditional

Table 5-1

STATES WITH HIGH LEVELS OF
PARTICIPATION IN AGRARIAN DEBATE

State	Percentage of all Speeches Year			Total Agrarian Measures Proposed
	1962	1963	1964	
Pernambuco...................	11.9	(4.0)	(5.5)	2
Minas Gerais.................	14.3	13.1	18.2	2
Rio de Janeiro..............	(2.4)	10.1	3.6	2
Guanabara...................	(4.8)	12.1	5.5	2
São Paulo...................	16.7	10.0	10.9	4
Rio Grande do Sul..........	16.7	13.1	14.5	1
Total 6 states........	66.8	62.4	58.2	13
Other 18 states............	33.2	37.6	41.8	3
Total..................	100	100	100	16

In addition to the states included in Table 5-1, there were several other states that fulfilled one or the other of the criteria for selection into this table. Paraná contributed 10.9% of all speeches in 1964, but no member of its delegation made any agrarian related proposals or motions. Espírtu Santo and Goiás, while falling short of the 10% minimum both have records of their representatives making agrarian related proposals (one in Espírtu Santo, and two in Goiás).

172

latifundia (Minas Gerais, and Pernambuco).[4] However insufficient any one demographic indicator may be for explaining intensity of involvement in the debate, the focus on an underlying political rationale appears to be well founded.

All states were, in fact, immediately and acutely concerned with the _political_ consequences of both land reform and of the agrarian reform debate. This political interest in land reform seemed to be strongly related to a growing politicization of the population based on social mobilization, and on a trasitional phase of agricultural development.

The six states with the most active delegations experienced a high degree of social and political mobilization in the years during and immediately preceding the land reform debate. This mobilization expressed itself in political polarization and fragmentation, growth of minor, splinter parties, politicization of not only urban, but also of rural workers, and land invasions. The group consisted of precisely those states in which the _social_ and _political_ problems of agriculture were most pressing, and frequently the focus of national attention: e.g., the _ligas camponesas_ in Pernambuco, Brizola's radical land reform in Rio Grande do Sul, São Paulo's Agrarian Revision Law, and massive land invasions in Rio de Janeiro and Minas Gerais. As a city state, Guanabara did not quite fit the picture. The reasons for its activism must therefore be located in the political and ideological consequences of the growth of radical populist politics.

The politicization of the land reform issue, and the degree to which the issue took on political as opposed to economic importance is suggested by

the column of figures under the year 1963 in table
5-1. It was during this year, the heyday of political radicalism and populism, that Guanabara became
intensely involved in the agrarian debate. The very
highly politicized state of Rio de Janeiro found itself involved for similar reasons. The distribution
of figures suggests that in these states in particular, the motivation was highly political and related
to the context in which the debate developed during
João Goulart's presidency.

Among these six states a small subcategory consisting of Minas Gerais, São Paulo, and Rio Grande
do Sul demonstrated consistent, as opposed to non-
uniform, high levels of participation in the debate
for the period of analysis. Historically, the three
states had a great deal in common. São Paulo and
Minas Gerais, and to a lesser extent, Rio Grande do
Sul, were traditionally the most powerful states in
Brazil, especially during the days of the Old Republic and of the "politics of the governors." In all
three states, despite great differences in levels of
industrialization, commercial agriculture remained
a very important sector of the economy. São Paulo
is the center of Brazilian industrial development;
but it is also an important coffee producer, and
therefore, responsible for an important share of
Brazil's export earnings. In all three states, the
significance of agricultural organization lay not
only in its economic contribution but also in that it
served as the social basis for political control.
Implicitly, for all three states, and particularly
for Minas Gerais and Rio Grande do Sul, the maintenance of traditional elistist patterns of political
control constituted the hidden agenda of the land

reform controversy. São Paulo's slightly lowered
participation in 1963 and 1964 as compared to the
other two states may well be a consequence of the
fact that paulista agriculture was already relatively modern, while that of the other two states was
modernizing, and therefore somewhat more caught up
in a transition. As Samuel Huntington observed,
whereas modernity leads to stability, modernization
contributes to social and political unrest.[3] It is
therefore not at all surprising that the transitional states should be most concerned about the possible consequences of an agrarian reform in Brazil.

POLITICAL PARTY AFFILIATION AND ATTITUDES TOWARD LAND REFORM

Reflecting histories of eclectic constituency
acquisition, Brazilian political parties evolved as
pragmatic coalitions of local and state clienteles.
Constructed primarily to win elections and to provide a means of distributing the patronage and favors that come with power, parties possessed little
ideological coherence or programmatic unity. The
larger parties in particular housed a variety of interests and constituencies. Since the major parties
frequently drew on similar clienteles in building
electoral coalitions, there was considerable overlap
among them. For example, although the UDN stood
ideologically somewhat right of center, its bossa
nova section had much more in common with the moder-
ate-left Christian Democratic Party (PDC). The difficulty in determining a party's ideological position
was heightened in the case of the PSD. Its pragmatic, adaptive, and frequently opportunistic aggre-
gative behavior frequently belied the largely con-

175

servative attitudes held by the _coroneis_ in its rank
and file.

Given the nature of Brazilian parties, the use
of party affiliation as a means of establishing a
member's ideological convictions can be a somewhat
unreliable tool. Nevertheless, although by no means
paragrons of ideological rigor, Brazilian parties
could be located on a general continuum from right
conservative to left reformist. Thus, parties like
the Republic Party (PR) and the Liberal Party (PL)
were understood to be staunch supporters of the status quo and traditional political and social values,
while the Brazilian Socialist Party (PSB) and the
Workers Renovation Movement (MTR) at the other end of
the scale were commonly recognized as advocating fundamental social and economic reform in favor of the
working class. Such a political ranking of parties
in accordance with general ideological tendencies is
used in this section of analysis of the congressional debates as a means of identifying the degree to
which individual positions adopted on land reform
corresponded to the position of the party of membership and to that party's location on the political
spectrum.

The preceding chapter stressed the salience of
agrarian reform as an issue with considerable political and populist significance. Observable interest in the issue appeared to be strongly related to
a presidential strategy oriented toward reinforcing
his power base. Reciprocally, an equally strong conviction existed on the part of opposition parties in
Congress that the legislature must retain control of
the issue to prevent just such an accretion of what
it considered dangerous power to Jango. The mani-

pulation of the agrarian issue for strategic political reasons should consequently be reflected in the varying intensity of the congressional debates on land reform.

Table 5-2 shows participation in the debate by party members from 1962 to 1964. In addition to indicating how many deputies from the entire party delegation debated the issue, it also records the total number of speeches made by the participating members of a party. As expected, variation in rates of speech-making on land reform parallels the demagogic manipulation of radical populist issues as a means of securing and expanding mass political support. In 1962, land reform had been singled out as a key issue by the president and was recognized as such by the Congress. Neither was inclined, however, to press for a concrete policy decision on the matter at this point. Both president and representatives made bland statements favoring land reform, but were careful to avoid sounding too enthusiastic or clear on the particulars of the issue. The radicalization of Brazilian politics and the key importance of land reform in this process were more clearly discernible in the 1963 debates. Whereas in 1962, only 42 deputies, or the total of 12.8 percent made speeches on land reform, almost three times the number, or 25.6 percent, debated the issue in 1963. Not only were there more deputies involved and more speeches made, but there was also a particularly sharp increase in the participation of members of small radical left wing parties. These parties ceased to figure prominently in the agrarian debate in 1964 as the result of the inhibiting effect the revolution had on their membership and activities. In fact, there was an overall de-

177

Table 5-2

DEPUTY PARTICIPATION IN AGRARIAN REFORM DEBATE, BY PARTY AND BY YEAR

Political Party	1960 Election	1962 Debate		1962 Election	1963 Debate		1964 Debate	
		Deputies	Speeches		Deputies	Speeches	Deputies	Speeches
PRP..........	3	1	1	2	1	6	1	3
PR...........	17	2	4	10	3	1	2	3
PSP..........	25	5	11	23	3	4	1	1
PL...........	3	1	1	5	3	10	1	1
UDN..........	70	6	9	97	36	71	20	43
PSD..........	115	8	10	119	15	23	14	26
PDC..........	6	6	7	19	8	15	5	7
PTB..........	66	11	14	104	29	47	14	23
PTN..........	7	–	–	11	1	1	–	–
PST..........	2	1	1	6	1	2	1	2
PSB..........	10	1	1	5	2	5	–	–
MTR*.........	–	–	–	4	3	5	1	2
PTR**........	2	–	–	3	–	–	–	–
Total........	326	42	59	409	105	190	60	111
% of Total...		12.8			25.6		14.6	
Speeches/ Deputy.......			1.4			1.8		1.8

* The MTR participated in elections for the first time in October 1962, and therefore did not participate in the debate in 1962.

** Since no deputies from the PRT participated in the debate, it is excluded from all further discussion in this study.

178

cline in the agrarian debates in 1964. Speech making
fell by 11 percent from 1963. Speechmaking on agriculture remained above the 1962 level, but this might
have reflected not only sustained interest in land
reform but also the fact that between the 1960 and
1962 elections the Chamber grew by eighty-three additional seats as the result of a general increase in
the Brazilian population.

A principal concern of this study is the determination of what the attitudes of deputies and parties were on agrarian reform itself, and the extent
to which certain political parties might have adopted particular positions for strategic as opposed to
ideological reasons. The following analysis dis-
criminates between these two concerns, and arrives at
an estimation of party position and ideological inclination towards potential reform of the land tenure
system and, by extension, of power in Brazil. One
means of discriminating among attitudes of deputies
who insisted they were in favor of an agrarian reform was to identify what the concept meant to them
and whether they understood it to be an economic
measure to fine tune a given situation, or whether
they perceived it as a measure of social reform.

Table 5-3 indicates a positive relationship
between perceptions of agriculture as both an economic and social problem. The two definitions of
agrarian reform are complementary primarily from the
perspective of social reform which accepts economic
measures as part of a general strategy. The reverse,
however, is not true. Approximately one third of
those contending that agriculture was an economic
problem rejected the social definition of the issue
and insisted on economic solutions and aimed at in-

179

Table 5-3

DEPUTY PERCEPTION OF AGRARIAN PROBLEM, BY PARTY

Political Party	Total	Agrarian Problem is Economic			Agrarian Problem is Social		
		Number	% of Party	% of Total	Number	% of Party	% of Total
PRP...........	1	1	100.	.9	0	0.	0.
PR............	3	1	33.3	.9	1	33.3	1.5
PSP...........	4	4	100.	3.6	3	100.	4.6
PL............	4	3	75.	2.7	2	50.	3.1
UDN...........	33	26	78.8	23.4	8	34.8	12.3
PSD...........	27	18	66.7	16.2	7	33.3	10.8
PDC...........	12	11	91.7	9.9	6	75.	9.2
PTB...........	40	40	100.	36.	31	93.9	47.7
PTN...........	1	1	100.	.9	1	100.	1.5
PST...........	2	2	100.	1.8	2	100.	3.1
PSB...........	2	2	100.	1.8	2	100.	3.1
MTR...........	2	2	100.	1.8	2	100.	3.1
Total........	131	111	84.7	100.	65	63.7	100.

creasing productivity. The margin of difference between those arguing for economic or for social solutions is widest for some of the larger parties: the
PSD, the UDN, the conservative Liberal Party (PL),
the moderate left Christian Democratic Party (PDC),
and the right populist Social Progressive Party (PSP).

As a means of checking on the sincerity of those
who felt that land reform was a social necessity, general support for land reform was compared to support
for the constitutional amendment which could make
such a policy effective.   Table 5-4 indicates a fair
degree of congruity between these two criteria.   The
overall difference in the figures on the two categories
is relatively small. Only 7.9 percent of those favoring land reform bills seemed inclined to oppose an
amendment.   A closer look at figures for individual
parties reveals a few anomalies, such as the fact
that within the UDN a greater percentage actually
came out in support of an amendment than in favor of land
reform.   Since the assessment was based in some part
on an inclination to approve the Castelo amendment,
further comment on this point will await the discussion of the impact of the political milieu on the interpretation of the land reform issue.

The most significant information rendered by
table 5-4 is that, given a general ranking of political parties from conservative (top) to reformist
(bottom), a favorable attitude toward agrarian reform is not as reliable an indicator of ideological
persuasion as is the attitude toward the amendment.
The figures on the two criteria substantiate the
contention that agrarian reform was for many deputies, especially for those from center and conservative parties, an exploitable political issue whose use-

Table 5-4

RELATIONSHIP OF ATTITUDES TOWARD
AN AGRARIAN LAW AND ATTITUDES TOWARD
AN AMENDMENT: DISTRIBUTION WITHIN PARTIES

Political Party	Expresses Support For			
	Agrarian Reform Bill		Payment for Land in Bonds	
	%No	%Yes	%No	%Yes
PRP................	100.0	–	100.0	–
PR.................	75.0	25.0	100.0	–
PSP................	25.0	75.0	60.0	40.0
PL.................	50.0	50.0	66.7	33.3
UDN................	76.2	23.8	76.0	25.0
PSD................	62.5	37.5	75.0	25.0
PDC................	30.0	70.0	22.2	77.8
PTB................	2.7	97.3	5.1	97.9
PTN................	–	100.0	–	100.0
PST................	–	100.0	–	100.0
PSB................	33.3	66.7	–	100.0
MTR................	33.3	66.7	–	100.0
Total.............	45.0	55.0	–	48.1

Direction of axis: Upper left (conservative) to lower right (reformist).

fulness ended at the point it actually threatened the existing distribution of economic and political power.

When a coefficient of association is calculated for the two variables (support for land reform and support for the amendment), the results in table 5-5 demonstrate that there is a high degree of positive association between the two (Gamma 917). Furthermore, using Guttman's coefficient of association, it is clear that the attitude on the amendment

(Lambda a) constitutes a better measure of predic-
tion of attitudes on land reform than vice versa.

An assessment of ideological attitudes on land
reform and on the constitutional amendment may contribute to a better understanding of party behavior
during the agrarian reform debate, but it does not
succeed in explaining this behavior entirely or ac-
counting for the high degree of variation in party
behavior in reference to unchanging principles or
ideological implications of a given policy. To explain such ideological inconstancy, additional information must be sought in the context within which the

Table 5-5

MEASURE OF ASSOCIATION BETWEEN ATTITUDES ON NEED
FOR AGRARIAN REFORM AND FOR CONSTITUTIONAL AMENDMENT

Constitutional Amendment	Agrarian Reform is Necessity			
	Number		% of Total	
	No	Yes	No	Yes
Against:				
any constitutional change..................	40	3	57.1	4.4
any change affecting property................	26	0	37.1	0
For:				
when socially necessary...............	2	49	2.9	72.1
politically necessary................	2	16	2.9	23.5
Total...................	70	68	100.0	100.0

Coefficients of Association: Gamma 91.7; Lambda a: 89.7;
Lambda b: 43.7; Lambda: 63.9.

agrarian debate develops. Two elements in particular
seem to exercise an appreciable influence over the
willingness of deputies to maintain or abandon a political posture. One is the deputies' estimation of

183

whether the president in power at the time is trustworthy and competent. The other is the opportunistic
urge to barter principles for power by engaging in
political accommodation with perceived sources of
power, be they issues or people. The struggles of
the political parties for an advantage in the electoral arena by capitalizing on the land reform issue
is a case in point.

The importance of these two elements can be perceived by comparing the final vote on the Goulart-PTB
amendment proposal, and on the Castelo amendment
proposal (table 5-6). Although differing in the
scope of their provisions, both amendments were identical in their purpose of altering the constitution
to make possible payment for expropriated land in
bonds instead of cash. In spite of this similarity,
the former proposal was defeated, and the latter
approved. It is true enough that the total number
of votes needed for the passage of the amendment in
a single session was reduced from 272 to 205. However, the totals also indicate that if the previous
rules for amending the constitution had been in effect the Castelo measure might never have been approved in 1964. Even so, it is significant that some
one hundred deputies, most from the UDN and PSD,
switched their votes from one year to the next, while
the PTB remained steadfast in its reformist inclinations. Not all who had opposed the Goulart agrarian
package switched, of course. In Último de Carvalho's
words, a few deputies remained "defenders of democracy." Still, the sincerity of deputies purported-
ly categorically against any type of constitutional
change is questionable. PTB deputy Fernando Gama
noted the inconsistency in the behavior of deputies

184

Table 5-6

VOTE ON THE CONSTITUTIONAL AMENDMENT

Political Party	1963 (Goulart)			1964 (Castelo)		
	Yes	No	Total	Yes	No	Total
PRP.....................	0	5	5	0	2	2
PR......................	0	3	3	1	2	3
PSP.....................	5	5	10	14	1	15
PL......................	0	3	3	1	0	1
UDN.....................	1	72	73	51	11	62
PSD.....................	5	69	74	63	12	75
PDC.....................	6	10	16	12	2	14
PTB.....................	87	0	87	79	1	80
PTN.....................	6	3	9	2	1	3
PST.....................	7	0	7	3	2	5
PSB.....................	4	0	4	2	0	2
MTR.....................	1	2	3	2	0	2
Subtotal...............	121	172	293	220	34	254
Recorded Abstentions...			3			1
Total..................			296			255
Official Total*........	121	176	297	232	33	265

*The count, by party, was tallied for both years from the offi-
cial roll call in the Anais da Câmara and the Diário Nacional
do Congresso, respectively. There are some obvious discrep-
ancies between the final official declaration at the end of
the vote, and the voting record reproduced in the official publications. The discrepancy may be explained in part by errors
in recording (failure to record certain votes, or to record
properly the votes of all deputies). Such an explanation perhaps is more applicable to the 1963 vote than to 1964. In the
case of the latter, there is a possibility that the difference
of ten votes may be accounted for by pairing.

who almost unanimously approved the constitutional
amendment to put the land tax in the hands of the município authorities, yet insisted, when it came to land reform and expropriation, that they could not countenance
any type of constitutional reform whatsoever.[5]

Few deputies were forthright about the type of
amendment they would support, and what type they
would vote against. Earlier discussion of congressional politics (chapter 4) noted the reservations
many deputies had about the Goulart-PTB amendment,
and the possibility that more deputies might have
supported the amendment if it had been more moderate.
The reverse is also true. Some deputies declined to
support either the Goulart or Castelo amendment because they were not radical enough. In 1963, the
Workers Renovation Movement withheld support from
the Goulart measure, not because it was against an
amendment, but because it felt that Goulart's flag-
ging interest and decision to withdraw from the debate jeopardized chances for serious reform.[6] In another vein, Geremias Fontes, a member of the Chris-
tain Democratic Party who was to become governor of
the state of Rio de Janeiro in 1966, argued that his
party should not support the 1964 Castelo amendment
proposal because it gave too much of an advantage to
the large landowners.[7]

Not all deputies pegged their support of a constitutional amendment to the political and personal
identity of the presidential incumbent. There was
also an unwavering core of opposition to changing
articles 141 and 146 of the constitution which survived into the Castelo administration. Jaeder
Albergara, one of the few deputies to vote against
the amendment in 1964 pointed out that, ironically,

the land reform issue had weighed heavily in the decision to depose Goulart. In retrospect, he wonder-
ed why they had gone to so much trouble to oust Jango
when the final outcome for the agrarian sector was to
be the same.[8] Último de Carvalho, who also voted
against the measure, questioned what assurance there
would be that the successor to the Castelo regime
would live up to the seriousness of Castelo's promises and intentions? Furthermore, he asked, what if
Goulart were to return by some chance, to find the
right to property violated by the "hands of the
democrats themselves?"[9]

Table 5-7

WILLINGNESS TO TRUST THE GOVERNMENT
WITH AGRARIAN REFORM

Political Party	Regime							
	Goulart				Castelo			
	Number		% of Party		Number		% of Party	
	No	Yes	No	Yes	No	Yes	No	Yes
UDN..........	38	5	88.4	11.6	12	9	57.1	42.9
PSD..........	17	5	77.8	22.7	6	5	54.5	45.5
PDC..........	3	7	30.0	70.0	4	4	50.0	50.0
PTB..........	1	40	2.4	97.6	1	18	5.3	97.7
Total......	59	57	50.9	49.1	23	36	39.0	61.0
Total all Parties....	73	67	52.1	47.9	26	38	40.6	59.4

The political sponsorship of the agrarian package and personal confidence in the president clearly
weighed a great deal in the minds of many deputies.
Table 5-7 offers some suggestion of how the members
of major parties viewed the two presidents' ability

to handle the agrarian reform responsibilities. The
PTB consistently remained supportive of the agrarian
issue, even if it were implemented by another administration. On the other hand, both the PSD and the
UDN obviously had greater confidence in putting land
reform in the hands of Castelo Branco than in those
of João Goulart.

Assuming that support of the consitutional
amendment, regardless of who proposed it, was the
most accurate indication of ideological position,
basic attitudes on the amendment were crosstabulated
with attitudes reflecting the degree to which the
political identity of the government in power influenced the final decision of the deputies on the
amendment.

Table 5-8

RELATIONSHIP OF ATTITUDE TOWARD PRESIDENT
AND ATTITUDE TOWARD AMENDMENT

Favors Amendment	Government is Important			
	No	Yes	Total	% Total
No....................	25	24	49	47.6
Yes...................	26	28	54	52.4
Total...............	51	52		
% Total.............	54	46	103	100

Table 5-8 indicates that only 25 percent of the
deputies in the sample were categorically against the
amendment regardless of which government was in power
at the time. Only a slightly greater percentage
would have voted for an amendment regardless of who
was in power. In other words, approximately one half

of all the deputies in the sample made their vote conditional on the identity, both political and personal, of the incumbent president.

The above table is based on and well illustrated by examples of discussions from the Chamber debates. For instance, Deputy Brito Velho, a member of the Liberal Party from Rio Grande do Sul, was known as a long time supporter of land reform. Yet, in the discussions of the Goulart proposal, he indicated that he would vote against the amendment (as indeed he did when the time came). When accused by other deputies of being a turncoat, he defended himself against the charge by saying he not only favored an amendment, but that he had even drafted an amendment proposal himself. At this point, PTB deputy Alceu de Carvalho accused Brito Velho of lacking confidence in the government's ability to carry out a land reform. Brito concurred: "/I have/ very strong doubts in regard to its capability."[10] Udenista Taurino Dantas echoed these sentiments when he said he was less concerned with how expropriated land would be paid for, than he was with putting land reform in the hands of an inept and politically opportunistic government.[11] Another congressman who opposed the Goulart proposals remarked to me in an interview that the Goulart-PTB proposal had its merits, but could not be entrusted to that regime which in his view consisted of a "gang of illiterate leftist demagogues."

SUPRA, the agrarian reform agency, came in for a heavy share of the blame for contributing to the Goulart administration's untrustworthy image by encouraging unrest in the countryside. Cid Furtado lamented that "administrative organs like SUPRA, which are urgently needed, are extremely suspect because

of the /radical7 ideology of various persons holding
directing positions."[12] Assailing the administration's
knowledge of real conditions in the countryside,
Geraldo de Pina alleged that João Pinheiro Neto was
unqualified for the job and unfamiliar with its subject matter. "It is likely," he charged, "/that he7
has never seen a rice plantation, or heard the lowing
of an ox. . . ."[13]

The trustworthiness of the president and his
aides was not the only issue at stake in the decision
to provide or withdraw support from certain measures.
Another important consideration, although the reading
of the data is not as clear on this point, was the
identity of the political party authoring or sponsoring a particular measure. In order to get some
indication of the relationship between attitudes on
the Goulart-PTB amendment and attitudes on other
measures discussed in the Chamber, attitudes on the
Goulart-PTB amendment were run against attitudes on
the Campos bill, the PSD-PTB compromise amendment,
the Badra bill, and Castelo Branco's agrarian bill.
Table 5-9 does bear out to some degree the contention
that political opportunism in the guise of electoral
maneuvering played a key role in political decisions
in Congress. In their most essential lines the
Campos, Badra, and Castelo (Land Statute) bills were
quite similar, yet the reaction to them differed.
The PTB and other left wing parties which were committed to land reform were less likely to allow the
party sponsorship in Congress and the identity of the
president to influence them against a particular
measure than were the conservative parties. Also,
judging by the success of the Badra bill, it appears
that the radical character of a proposal was not

Table 5-9

ASSOCIATION BETWEEN ATTITUDE TOWARD THE GOULART-PTB
AMENDMENT, AND ATTITUDES TOWARD OTHER AGRARIAN BILLS

Approves	Approves Goulart-PTB Amendment		
	No	Yes	Total
Campos Bill			
No......................	8	29	37
Yes.....................	37	10	47
PSD-PTB Amendment and Bill			
No......................	60	1	61
Yes.....................	10	35	45
Badra Bill			
No......................	4	16	20
Yes.....................	24	10	34
Castelo Amendment and Bill			
No......................	30	2	32
Yes.....................	15	49	64

necessarily a determining factor for the PTB and the
left which voted for the Castelo land reform package in
1964. At this point, the passage of the measures was
assured not only by an alteration in the procedure
for amending the constitution, but also very substantially by the decision of members of conservative
parties to change their position and vote for the
amendment. The change of attitude by Congress as a
unit reflect not so much a change of heart on land
reform, as it did the installation of a new regime
regarded as more trustworthy by conservative parties.

The change in the behavior of the deputies was
not necessarily an indication of ideological betrayal. On the contrary, as Milton Rokeach has pointed
out, "an attitude object is always encountered within

some situation, about which we also have an organized attitude."[14] In the final analysis, "behavior is a function of the interaction between the two types of attitudes."[15]

No doubt, under any circumstances, the importance ascribed by Brazilian parties to contextual political circumstances surrounding policy issues would be considered high. If the land reform debate serves as a valid example of the manner in which substantive issues are approached and deliberated, then the importance of the political context is even greater than indicated by the figures. The distortion of an issue by immediate political influences is compounded by the nature of the communication process in political discussion. During the discussions of land reform in the Chamber, the deputies seemed to talk past each other, perhaps to unseen audiences rather than to each other. Knowledge of issues, and substantive information about rural conditions and their implication were sorely lacking. As a result, since reliable information about the "attitude object," or issue, was unavailable, the importance of the context in determining operative attitudes increased accordingly. Ultimately, the final decision was determined in great part by the degree of confidence in the stability of the political situation and the relative trustworthiness of the government. A few examples from the debate will suffice to illustrate the point.

In arguing their position on land reform, the deputies frequently cited examples from Brazil and other areas of the world to substantiate their claims. Because their knowledge of the economics and social conditions anywhere was, by and large, shallow, their exchanges were frequently reduced to diatribes which to the observer seemed comic at times. A favorite ploy of the left, which spent a good portion of its time fending off charges of dangerous radicalism and sympathy for communism, was to cite in its defense the views or remarks of such unimpeachable democrats as John F. Kennedy, Lord Hume, various Brazilian bishops, and even Nelson Rockefeller.[16] This strategy occasionally backfired, as when conservative PSD member Peixoto da Silveira lashed out against land reform and any of its supporters regardless of how impeccable their democratic credentials. The Alliance for Progress and the speeches of President Kennedy on land reform, he insisted, had the sole objective of keeping Brazil essentially agricultural, colonial, and poor.[17] On another occasion when the subject of an internal communist threat was revived, this time to warn that Brazil might follow in the footsteps of the Soviet Union, socialist deputy and scholar Guerreiro Ramos provided the Chamber with a detailed analysis assuring the deputies that according to marxist theory this was not about to happen. Brazil had yet to pass through a phase of capitalist development which required the elimination of a semi-feudal landowning pattern.[18]

In conclusion, the analysis of the debates in the Chamber of Deputies generally bears out previous observations about political party behavior during the agrarian debate. Ultimately, the strategies and the behavior of political parties reflected their perception and interpretation of the political situation and of their relationship to the government in power. This was particularly true of the PSD, although the other parties by no means escaped the tinge of this type of pragmatism and opportunism.

Ideology, however, was not totally irrelevant.
Although political party attitudes and behavior did
undergo some modification from one set of political
circumstances to another, there existed an undercur-
rent of firm opinion on the agrarian issue (i.e.,
attitude toward object) that remained largely unmod-
ified over the years of the debate. The best example
of this was the mineiro wing of the PSD and the UDN,
as well as the ideological core of the PTB.

The lasting impression of political interaction
in the Brazilian Congress is that of a clientelistic
marketplace where certain commodities may never come
up for sale or barter, but where many others are
traded off cannily by the shrewed political merchants,
always on the lookout for a political bargain or a
new contact. The picture also has some of the characteristics of an elaborate stage production where
roles are played and lines recited in an opera buffa.
In the dramatic ritual, elaborate eulogies about the
personal characteristics of a certain "noble, wise,
learned, esteemed, and virtuous" colleague are transformed into vehicles of personal insult and political
vendetta. One has the impression that the self importance of the actors is a reflection of the absence
of a stage director or of a consensus among the actors
on how the play is to be concluded. In the case of
land reform in Brazil, the sobering reality was reintroduced with the military coup which, while appearing
initially to bear out the desires of the actors,
eventually caused them to recite from a new script.

NOTES

1. See the Appendix for a reproduction of the code and methodological note.

2. Mato Grosso appears as prominent as it does because of a small but very active delegation. All demographic information is based on 1960 figures taken from the Anuário Estatístico.

3. Huntington, Ch. 5, "Revolution and the Political Order, pp. 264-343.

4. By emphasizing one type of agricultural activity in a certain state, we do not mean to imply that others do not exist. Minas Gerais also has commercial agriculture and São Paulo, latifundia.

5. Fernando Gama, PTB, Paraná, Anais, Vol. VII, 1963, 49 ses., May 27, 824.

6. Derville Alegretti, MTR-São Paulo, Anais, Vol. XI, 158 ses., Sept. 10, pp. 599-604.

7. Anais, Vol. XXVIII 1964, 206 ses., Oct. 26, p. 492.

8. Albergara, PSD, Minas Gerais, Anais, Vol. XXX 1964, 218 ses., Nov. 9, pp. 560-61.

9. Anais, Vol. XXVIII 1964, 202 ses., Oct. 21, p. 692.

10. Anais. Vol. VII, 1963, 47 ses., May 22, p. 607.

11. Anais, Vol. XII, 1963, 89 ses., July 2, p. 707.

12. Anais, Vol. VI, 1963, 38 ses., May 13, p. 419.

13. Anais, Vol. I, 1963/1964, 7 ses., Jan. 17, p. 358.

14. Milton Rokeach, Belief, Attitudes, and Values (San Francisco: Jossey-Bass, Inc., 1969), p. 119.

15. Ibid., pp. 127-8.

16. See, for example, Chagas Rodrigues, Anais, Vol. VI, 1963, 37 ses., May 10, pp. 251-56.

17. Anais, Vol. XXIX 1963, 178 ses., Sept. 24, pp. 199-203.

18. Anais, Vol. XI, 1963, 157 ses., Sept. 10, p. 555.

6. The Policy Process and Conservative Modernization

Success in policy making rests in a mastery of the rules of the game, or alternatively, the ability to redefine them. In either case, skillful pursuit of policy objectives requires a sensitive appreciation of both the possibilities for change and the limitations on reform imposed by existing institutions and interests.[1] Jango's failure to achieve his agrarian program was directly related to his misperception and even disregard of the limitations on his policy choices within the existing framework. On the other hand, Castelo's ability to secure a land reform law must be understood not only as the result of wiser political craft and more propitious circumstances, but also of prudent observance of the policy constraints imposed by influential conservative elites.

In the case of Brazil, as in most Latin American countries, the viability of a sweeping redistributive policy would have required one of two preconditions. First, either through revolution or gradual attrition, the power of established elites would have had to be significantly weakened and that of new reformist and mass based leadership proportionately enhanced. Alternatively, such a policy would have required decisive support from a left-wing, reformist military acting in opposition to established social

and economic interests. Unlike Cuba, an example of
the first case, or Peru, an example of the second,
Brazil had neither a revolution, nor a nationalist
reformist military in control of the country. Behind the populist reformist façade of the Goulart administration, conservative interests retained their
control of traditional political institutions and
the support of the armed forces. Furthermore, despite the sympathy of some military officers for Basic
Reforms, the revolutionary features of Jango's policy
goals were perceived by the majority of the military
leadership as a threat to some of their primary objectives. Most importantly, in their view, an emphasis on redistributive social justice and high
rates of social mobilization would hinder the emergence of Brazil as a major world power and impair
national security by inviting Communist infiltration.
As demonstrated by the record of the post 1964 administrations, the armed forces decided that both
objectives required the consolidation of a sophisticated military and industrial capability founded on
a program of capital intensive development, diversification, and systematic national integration and
centralization. While not precluding reforms, this
program required that any new agrarian policy be
subordinate to the general political and economic
goals of a modernizing conservative leadership.

STRATEGY AND STYLE IN POLICY MAKING

With respect to land reform, there were clear
limitations on the type of program that Brazil's
corporatist establishment was willing to tolerate,
and Jango's proposals fell beyond the limits of its
toleration. But to ascribe his failure to achieve an

agrarian reform program to a monolithic reactionary opposition is too simplistic an explanation. It assumes on the part of the latifundistas an unrealistic degree of power and sway over other interest sectors and attributes to the Brazilian policy process a rigid ideological character that is belied by a history of pragmatic, incremental decision making within a conservative framework.

Evidence gathered from interviews and published sources suggests that industrial and commerical elites had little understanding or sympathy for the problems of their counterparts in the agrarian sector.[2] However, they quickly discovered compelling reasons to be concerned for the landowners' problems when Goulart used land reform as a political threat not merely against traditional latifundia owners, but also against all established economic interests. Furthermore, once denied routine access to the presidency and to opportunities for negotiating over policies affecting their perceived domain, these interests were unified. Bound by their perception of a common threat, they resorted, in effect, to a residual veto power by deposing the offending administration.

Earlier in this study, the discussion of how Brazilian interest groups impact the policy process pointed out their relatively ineffective lobby activity, lack of organization, and absence of reliable knowledge and meaningful communication within and among their associations. In an interest structure both highly fragmented and weighted in the president's favor, specific interests have had considerable difficulty preserving their concerns against executive determination to pursue particular policy

goals. This was evident, for example, in the case
of the supposedly powerful agricultural sector (especially the coffee growers), which acquiesced to de
facto subsidy of industrialization during the Vargas
dictatorship. Even within "democratic" periods,
which encouraged decentralization and regionalism
and permitted greater exercise of interest group
pressure, the Brazilian president could wield considerable power over policy through the use of clientelistic benefits, patronage, and the manipulation of
dependent corporatist organizations. Corporatism
and clientelism, by preserving personalistic, dyadic
loyalty and interest fragmentation, enhanced executive power at the expense of developing effective
interest articulation by grass roots organization.
However, elite interests collectively retained a decisive control over the framework within which the
policy process took place. The power of the state,
as expressed through the executive, lay in its legitimacy as a mediator of interest and an arbiter of
conflicts within an established elite biased framework. Jango undermined his own legitimacy not because he challenged a particular interest, but because he in effect attacked its source, the fundamental political framework itself.

From this perspective, Leff's provocative interpretation of executive discretion and decision making
power may be viewed as both insightful and deficient.[3]
His observations on four cases of economic policy
making pertain primarily to circumstances in which
the president successfully and safely played by the
rules of the game. His conclusions provide little
basis for understanding the process of a policy issue
like land reform, which, contrary to established

practice could not be contained by the deliberations of executive bureaucrats, but instead overflowed into a passionate and widespread public debate abetted by presidential design. In E. E. Schattschneider's terminology, Jango, like Vargas before him, was trying to prevail with his policies by "socializing" the conflict over the issue.[4] He was, in other words, attempting to redefine the balance of power in the political system by expanding the field of participants and tipping the balance in his favor. But Getúlio's shrewd cultivation of the urban working class was an adjunct of a development plan that reinforced the corporatist political framework and served the interests of the growing industrial sector. Moreover, it enjoyed the support of the military and even, reluctantly, of the middle class liberals. In contrast, Jango's strategy for welding a new reformist political coalition gained few friends and made powerful enemies. From the beginning, his strategy fatally overestimated the strength and constancy of his populist allies and underestimated the resourcefulness and determination of his corporatist opposition, its ability to respond decisively to a threat, and to secure the sympathy of the armed forces.

Jango's performance in the executive office evinced profound frustration over the contradictory pressures created by imposing a populist representative democracy on a corporatist authoritarian framework. Possessed of neither the propitious circumstances nor the political astuteness of Juscelino Kubitschek, Jango found the simplicity of sweeping revolutionary reforms an irresistable course of action. As Hirschman observed in his discussion of

land reform in Colombia, "revolution requires 'only'
the violent overthrow of certain ruling groups. . .
whereas reform requires a special combination of circumstances, a sequence of moves in the course of
which the ruling groups acquiesce to, or even connive
in, the nibbling away of their own privileges."[5]
Jango aggravated rather than lessened his policy problems by insisting that the ruling groups acquiesce
not merely to the "nibbling away of their own privileges," but to allowing the lower class to gobble up
the whole pie.

To some extent, then, Jango's failure to achieve
his policy goals seems the product of a self fulfill-
ing prophecy. His comprehensive reform approach reflected two important errors of judgment. It denied
the possibility that reforms could be introduced in-
crementally and overestimated the political strength
of the manipulated lower class as a counterweight to
the power of conservative interests and established
institutions. By approaching agrarian policy as if
Brazilian society consisted of a small exploitative
and backward landed elite on the one hand and a mass
of landless workers on the other, Jango imputed to
the decision making structure an unrealistic degree
of monolithic inflexibility and an inability to accommodate reform of any kind. Under such circumstances, the land reform debate was cast as a revolutionary struggle, short of which no progress or
alteration of the rural status quo could be achieved.

Yet, in fact, Brazilian society was complex and
varied, and the corporatist establishment far from
monolithic or unified until the issue became ideologically defined as an uncompromising struggle between
the masses and the exploiters. The coroneis of the

PSD, the party most representative of traditional landed interests, were willing to negotiate with Jango over an agrarian policy package that would, in fact, have been more reformist than that finally secured by Castelo. But Jango was ultimately unwilling to compromise or connive to make the landowners participants in their own transformation. He firmly supported the PTB position, which dichotomized society into two oppositing parties and consequently polarized political leadership into those for and against Goulart. In this highly politicized and ideologically inflamed situation negotiation and compromise were effectively precluded.

In contrast, Humberto Castelo Branco enjoyed two distinct and important advantages in his effort to achieve a land reform law based on a constitutional amendment. One was that changes in institutional relations and in the political climate had increased the power of the presidency. The powers of the executive were not yet as sweeping as they would be after the fifth institutional act of 1968, which trimmed the Congress of its remaining powers and eliminated for the military government the bothersome vestiges of the democratic era. But Castelo clearly enjoyed greater leverage with Congress than had Jango. He also enjoyed the confidence of conservative interests and at that point was generally supported in his efforts by the armed forces. The new political climate, achieved at the cost of a massive purge of left wing leaders and organizations and the suspension of basic human liberties, did not assure, however, a complete agreement among the victors. It did indicate an assumption that there existed an agreement on general goals and that negotiation was

203

possible over particulars. Accordingly, Castelo's second important advantage in the policy process was that his more conservative political objectives in agrarian reform assured greater support for his legislative measures, including the constitutional amendment. His circumspect proposals, therefore, provided a more realistic basis on which to negotiate with landowning interests.

Although important, these two advantages do not alone account for the successful passage of the law. Castelo's personal commitment to land reform played an important role in securing an early passage of the law and approval of the amendment. A special significance can be ascribed to his being a Northeasterner, the first Brazilian president from the Northeast since Epitácio Pessôa (1919-1922) and the second in Brazil's history. Equally important, Castelo expressed this commitment in a carefully articulated strategy. As described earlier, Castelo, his staff, and several cabinet ministers bargained, courted, explained, cajolled, and threatened. In the process, they were forced to concede several points. They emerged with a law that could not, as had been hoped, rely on the establishment of a separate system of rural justice to resolve agrarian conflicts and speed up the reform effort. They also had to accept a greater emphasis on colonization by agreeing to the establishment not only of IBRA, the Brazilian Institute of Agrarian Reform, but also of INDA, the National Institute of Agrarian Development.[6] Finally, they were left with a law which was riddled with contradictions and complexities and would possess little effectiveness without a strong presidential commitment behind it.

Nevertheless, they did achieve a law and the alteration of the constitution with the cooperation of a Congress dominated not by pro-reform interests (those had been purged and their political rights suspended), but by the retrograde interests of the UDN and the PSD. The new law did not signal the onset of an agrarian revolution in Brazil. But perhaps the point of this experience is that the Brazilian corporatist elites would not bow to a revolution or an overhaul of the land tenure system and were strong enough to prevent it. Any subsequent reform would therefore have to occur in an incremental fashion, if at all. Since 1964, land reform, as opposed to capitalist agrarian development, has been minimal. The problems in pursuing land reform occasioned by the weak law have been reinforced by administrations disinterested or hostile to egalitarian social objectives. But the existence of the law, the significance of the constitutional alteration of the terms governing the use of property, and the experiences in economic and social development attributable to the law's existence will constitute important stepping stones to a second agrarian phase which Brazil will, unavoidably, confront at some point in the future.

THE LAND STATUTE OF 1964

The despair of hard core conservatives who witnessed the passage of the constitutional amendment and land reform law was paralleled by the hope of reformists that these measures, although passed by an apparently conservative military regime, would bear the potential for beginning a land reform program in Brazil. Unquestionably, these contrary sentiments

205

were premised largely on the fact that the alteration of the constitution made possible the expropriation and redistribution of property without tying
that procedure to the availability of large reserves
of ready cash. These sentiments also seemed to be
based on an appreciation of the reformist determination of President Humberto Castelo Branco himself,
who had exercised considerable personal pressure to
secure the amendment's approval in the Congress and
who, during his brief administration (1964-1967),
accorded land reform a high priority. He appointed
Paulo Assiz Ribeiro, principal author of the new
law, to be the first director of the new Brazilian
Institute of Agrarian Reform, IBRA, and gave him the
rank of a cabinet minister. Moreover, IBRA was
accorded the status of superministry, enjoying a
priority among cabinet departments.[6] In 1965, reflecting this priority status, IBRA energetically
proceeded to carry out the first comprehensive cadastral survey of Brazil's immense territory and to
clear land titles. The completeness and reliability
of the outcome were questionable since they depended
on the declarations of the landowners themselves and
many large landowners declined to cooperate.[7] But
the measures were nevertheless an important first
step in providing more reliable information on the
land tenure system without which a knowledgeable reform effort could not proceed.[8]

Yet, most of the hopes and fears inspired by the
possibility of a sweeping reform of the land tenure
system were largely unfounded. According to Ribeiro,
although the constitutional amendment would facilitate expropriation, massive redistribution of property was not the purpose of the new legislation. "It

is not the large _fazenda_ we have fought," he emphasized; "it is the large unused property."[9] The
Castelo administration envisioned the law as a combination of economic and social measures which would
transform Brazilian agriculture into a modern and
productive sector of the economy and, in the process,
eliminate the acute and politically disruptive problems characteristic of traditional and transitional
rural areas. Large productive properties and agro-
industrial or commercial agricultural enterprises
were to be preserved and aided in their expansion
and development. Social tensions and conflicts resulting from the unavailability of farm land in problem areas would be alleviated through colonization
programs under the direction of INDA and, where
necessary, by the expropriation and redistribution of
unused or underutilized property and of minifundia.
Ostensibly, then, the law would encourage capitalist
development in the countryside both by eliminating
the latifundium and by transforming landless workers
and minifundia owners into middle class farmers. In
this respect the Land Statute bore a remarkable resemblance to the goals of the _sesmarias_ enacted six
centuries earlier by the Portuguese crown and applied
to colonial Brazil in its early developmental period.

In addition to establishing socially and politically conservative goals, the law itself constituted a weak instrument of economic reform. The cumbersome,lengthy statute (128 articles) met with
little praise from those looking for either technical
elegance and precision or for an effective instrument
with which to alter patterns of land use.[10] As Doreen
Warriner has pointed out, for maximum effectiveness,
an agrarian reform law must be clear in its objec-

207

tives, precise in the description of the procedures to be followed, and eschew vagueness, contradictions and complexity. The Land Statute, in contrast, was complex, confusing, and vague. Having no general application, it "required a number of administrative decisions before it could be implemented."[11] Rather than setting forth simple criteria by which land reform might be pursued, the law dedicated forty-two articles to explaining the mathematical equations by which the status and tax value of a property would be determined.[12] In its general vagueness and confusion, the new law conformed, in fact, to the Brazilian legal tradition which, Schmitter observed, served to "avoid a definitive point of closure," and allowed maximum room for reinterpretation in response to new political circumstances.[13] Or, as one Brazilian indicated in an interview apropos of the law, "Brazil has many laws, but it does not have one that says all the others have to be enforced."

Despite the hard battle for a constitutional amendment, the possibilities of expropriation were so limited as to be almost irrelevant. Although land itself could be paid for in bonds redeemable over a period of ten to twenty years (under Goulart the minimum was twenty years), all other property on the land, i.e., buildings, roads, dams, etc., required immediate payment in cash, even if they had been constructed by the government. In addition, the price of the land and all that was on it, regardless of its agricultural value, or increased value because of secondary construction, would be determined by the market and would, of course, be fully indexed for inflation. Under these circumstances, expropriation remained a

208

costly and difficult procedure and its implementation, it follows, would naturally be limited.

In addition to the inhibiting costs of expropriation, there were procedural obstacles to a general redistribution of property. Even highly unproductive properties were protected from expropriation
if they served as the site of a "rural industry."
The existence of a commercial enterprise, be it agricultural, stock raising, or agro-industrial in
nature on a latifundium, even if it occupied a mere
fraction of the land leaving the rest idle, was
enough to prevent expropriation of the unused portion.
Also,property which had been legally declared a latifundium could only be expropriated if it were located
in an officially designated "priority area" where
demand for land and conflict were high.[14]

The difficulties of expropriating unused land
did not end here. When IBRA decided which land in
preestablished "priority areas" should be expropriated, neither expropriation nor assumption of titles
by new owners was automatic. The owner retained the
right to challenge IBRA's decision in court. Until
the cumbersome Brazilian judicial system finally
ruled on the matter, the land remained in the owner's
control and several years might elapse before the
appeals procedure ran its course to an uncertain conclusion. Only then, assuming a favorable ruling on
the expropriation, could the land be distributed as
family farms to the camponeses. They then became
obligated to pay for the property over a twenty year
period, during which time they could not resell the
land.

It is not surprising, therefore, that the law

defined expropriation as a measure of last (and evidently uncertain) resort and designated progressive taxation as the major instrument of reform. With the exception of those properties located in priority areas which were declared expropriable, ununused, or underutilized, land was subject to a special land tax, the Impôsto Territorial Rural (ITR).[15] Its amount depended on the extent and value of the unused land, based on the declaration of the owner, and would increase yearly for five years up to a maximum rate of 2.7 percent. At that point, the property might be, but did not have to be expropriated. No stipulation existed that property assessments had to be indexed for inflation, as in the case of agrarian bonds. Since, for tax purposes, land in Brazil was notoriously undervalued and since inflation after the revolution remained over twenty percent a year, the tax on idle property appeared to large landowners to be more an annoyance than a believable threat.[16]

In addition to the above, the possible effectiveness of the land tax, ostensibly formulated to serve as the source of revenues to finance the agrarian program, was further undermined by constitutional restrictions on its use. Earlier, during the Goulart administration, the constitutional amendment of 1961 had transferred authority over land taxes from the federal government to the local municípios. The passage of Amendment 18 of December 1965 succeeded only partially in restoring federal authority over land taxation. The new amendment allowed the federal government to establish criteria for taxing property, but assigned collection authority to the states. These, in turn, were allowed to retain twenty percent of the proceeds, with the remainder returning to the

municípios. Lest this be perceived as a means of
developing local level agrarian reform efforts in
the possible absence of an effective federal initiative, the Land Statute specifically prohibited independent agrarian reform activity by state governments.

Nor were the problems of the land tax entirely
attributable to the exact provisions of the taxing
procedure or chronic inflation. Hirschman has observed that taxing idle or underutilized property is
one of the most ineffective ways to promote reform
and is best relegated to the category of "gadgetry."
At a minimum, the tax scheme requires realistic land
values based on a competent survey, and "is usually
found acceptable only when there is an imperious need
for new expenditures.[17] It is also a weak political
tool since "while it arouses the opposition of the
landed interests /and of small farmers as well/, it
does not hold out an obvious appeal to any other
important social group." In addition, the intended
beneficiaries of this policy, minifundia owners and
landless peasants, fail to perceive any direct relationship between tax measures and the possibility
that landowners may become more willing to sell or
rent land, or to lower their prices.[18]

The ambiguity and weakness of the law and the
circumspection with which it taxed landowners or expropriated idle property indicated that Brazil had
not yet acquired a reformist instrument which could
exploit the full potential of the amendment for im-
proving the lot of the camponeses. It was also clear
that in the absence of a forceful and independent
land reform authority, the law's application and effectiveness would depend greatly on the support it
received from the president. Yet, at this point in

211

Brazil's history, there was little expectation that the military presidents who were to succeed Castelo would share his social conscience or his conviction that land reform was one of Brazil's highest priorities. It is therefore not surprising that agrarian policy, particularly after 1967, has conformed closely to the priorities of conservative, state capitalist development and to the implicit limitations established by the corporatist elites' veto power over the scope and direction of reform.

AGRARIAN POLICY, 1965-1975

For Castelo, agrarian reform was a matter of deep personal commitment and he accorded it a high priority in his government. But the president's priorities outside the realm of economic stablization centered not on social reform itself, but rather, on the establishment of a new, stable, political process that would support economic development and technological change with seriousness and careful management. Behind a semiliberal façade, Castelo's authoritarian technocracy set about cleaning up corruption, subversion, and inefficiency. His dreams of limited democracy and popular support were dashed, however, by the gubernatorial elections of October 3, 1965. Instead of demonstrating, as desired, a widespread endorsement for the political and economic reforms of the past year and a half, the returns showed that the PSD led opposition, encouraged by former president Juscelino Kubitschek, continued to make a strong showing.

The electoral results triggered an internal coup by the linha dura (hard line military) who forced

Castelo to decree two more institutional acts, the
first of which, Institutional Act No. 2 of October
27, 1965, gave the government sweeping powers to sus-
pend political rights and try civilians in military
courts. Institutional Act No. 3 of February 5, 1966
provided for indirect election of governors, and the
appointment (as opposed to election, previously) of
mayors. A complementary act abolished the existing
party system and replaced it with an official two
party system in which ARENA, the National Renovating
Alliance, was established as the government party,
and the MDB, the Brazilian Democratic Movement, the
official opposition.

In the midst of the political crisis, sharpened
by already visible conflicts within the military as
to its future role in the government and on the policy objectives to be pursued, social reform objectives
faded from prominence. The hope for a serious attempt to apply the Land Statute, already overshadowed
by the internal coup of the linha dura and the succession struggle from which Minister of Defense
Arthur Costa e Silva would emerge victorious, was to
disappear with Castelo's departure from office.

Costa e Silva, from whom Brazil vainly awaited a
"humanization of politics," proved to be more rigid
and conservative than Castelo and less adept as a
leader. His laissez faire attitude toward what he
could not control or understand permitted factional
politics to reenter through the back door of his
regime. Social alienation increased and the deepening unrest and conflict with dissident social and
political groups ultimately led to another internal
coup. The result was an even more repressive military rule, known as well, if not better, the world

213

over for suppression of human rights and torture as for its economic achievements.

The watershed crisis of December 1968 arose when carioca federal deputy, Marcio Moreira Alves, publicly attacked the regime's terrorist tactics and its disregard for civil liberties. Congress' refusal to censure and strip him of political immunity provided the government with a pretext to proclaim Institutional Act No. 5 and close the national legislature. The linha dura was again able to force the hand of the president, much as it had done in 1967. The fifth institutional act extended even further the arbitrary powers of the executive. It renewed emphasis on cleaning up graft and corruption; on efficiency, purity, and morality; on centralization, administrative alignment of local with state and federal levels of government, and bureaucratic reform.

The stage was thus set for the next ten years of military government during which the armed forces could put into execution their vision of Brazil's economic and international future unrestrained by domestic bickering and subversive dissent. Within this context land reform was demoted from its priority status to take its place as a subordinate aspect of a comprehensive national strategy focusing on capitalist transformation and geographic and sectoral integration. Since 1968, the evolution of agrarian policy can be separated into three major aspects. These have consisted of the strengthening of the land reform law, the weakening of the administrative appartus that had been established to implement the law, and a close integration of agrarian policy with broader national development goals.

214

Reinforcement of the Land Statute

The determination of the military governments to bend all recalcitrant groups, including erstwhile allies, to the logic of Brazil's new economic order resulted in an anomalous strengthening of the provisions of the Land Statute. Armed with increased decree powers, President Costa e Silva was not required to appeal for congressional approval to revise the law. Instead, he issued a large number of decrees aimed at eliminating inefficient businesses and economically unproductive practices. Among these measures, Institutional Act Number Nine of April 25, 1969 increased the legal authority behind the Land Statute.[19]

First, it provided that the cost of expropriated land would no longer be determined by the market value of the property, but by the declared tax value of the land. Landowners were given exactly one hundred eighty days to submit final assessments on their properties. Land taxes in Brazil were by and large nonexistent before the revolution and, even after 1964, the declared value of the land for tax purposes was frequently a fraction of its real worth. The decree therefore aimed to catch the large landowners one way or another. If they declared the full value of their land, the government's tax revenues would increase; if they did not, their land, in theory, could be expropriated. Then they would receive no more than the undervalued sum that appeared on their tax declarations. To insure compliance with the registration of all properties at their actual worth, the decree required that landowners present a valuation certificate from the land tax office upon paying their income tax (another innovation of the revolu-

tionary government) as well as upon transacting any
legal and financial business concerning their property.

A second provision of the decree stipulated that
agrarian bonds would in the future be subject to a
maturation period of twenty years minimum and that
payment for expropriated property no longer had to be
made prior to the act of expropriation. This meant
that the state could take possession of the land
whether or not the owner agreed to the value of the
compensation. Disputes over the reimbursable value
of the land were to be reduced by fixing payment to
the value declared for tax purposes. The expropriation process was further streamlined by removing it
from the jurisdiction of the civil courts, and transferring authority over appeals and complaints to administrative offices.

These measures were a clear indication of the
government's impatience with the cumbersome machinery
established by the Land Statute to deal with and resolve conflictual rural problems. But if the ninth
institutional act was meant to increase the central
government's administrative authority, it should not
be interpreted as a sign of renewed reformist fervor
by the military regime. Indeed the organization reforms which accompanied the reinforcement of the land
law effectively redefined the emphasis of agrarian
policy by officially downgrading the agrarian reform
institute and minimizing still further the role of
land distribution in the overall agrarian policy.

Administrative Demotion of Land Reform

The administrative prominence of the land reform
effort had begun to suffer a decline even during the

Castelo Branco administration. Following the second inner coup of the _linha dura_ at the end of 1965, the priority of land reform gave way to more pressing political and economic concerns. As a consequence of an organizational reform in 1967, IBRA's director no longer held cabinet rank and, like the director of the agrarian development institute, INDA, now reported to the minister of agriculture instead of directly to the president.

The ninth institutional act of 1969 further blurred the distinction between the two organizations and increased their distance from the president. A number of functions that had previously been within the jurisdiction of INDA, such as colonization, were shifted to IBRA and both agencies were placed under a new administrative body, the Executive Group for Agrarian Reform, GERA, which was responsible to the minister of agriculture.

In addition to undermining its effectiveness and reducing its authority, IBRA's reorganization and frequent personnel changes also produced a negative impact internally causing a decline in morale and, eventually, the departure of some of its most dedicated staff to private industry. Originally they had to come to work at IBRA at lower salaries than those offered by the private sector because of their sense of commitment and hope that serious reform might indeed be implemented in Brazil. By 1969, in spite of the strengthening of the land reform law by the institutional act, there did not seem much point in staying on. One of these disillusioned staffers commented to me that IBRA had become "an atomic machine to make popcorn." There was no administrative authority and no political commitment from the nation's leadership to support the exercise of the increased powers and streamlined procedures of the new decree law.

By the third quarter of 1969 IBRA was no longer recognizable. The transfer of functions to it from INDA (essentially the result of personal rivalry between the minister of agriculture and the head of INDA) had reduced the agrarian reform institute to a functional copy of the Ministry of Agriculture. It was now required to deal not only with colonization, but also with extension programs, credit problems, and cooperatives. "The only thing that IBRA does not do," an irate and frustrated IBRA official fumed in an interview, "is distribute land." Debilitating politics seemed to have crept even into the one area where IBRA supposedly had jurisdiction: that of designating priority areas for land reform. IBRA's recommendations could be, and were regularly overruled by GERA. There were allegations that designation of priority areas was now motivated less by the existence of pressing rural problems than by the desire to use land reform as a gravy train for the allocation of public works and colonization projects.

The final step in the administrative demotion of land reform, represented graphically by table 6-1, occurred shortly thereafter. In October 1969, in a key speech on agrarian policy delivered in Rio Grande do Sul, Minister of the Interior Costa Cavalcanti stated that he firmly supported the existing agrarian structure and approved only of colonization as an acceptable strategy for dealing with the demand for land. The abolition of IBRA, INDA, and GERA by President Emilio Garrastazú Médici in mid 1970 and their replacement by a new autarchy, the National Institute

218

Table 6-1

STRUCTURE OF AUTHORITY OVER LAND REFORM

Year	Structure
1965	President ↓ IBRA
1967	President ↓ Minister of Agriculture ↓ IBRA
1969	President ↓ Minister of Agriculture ↓ GERA ↓ IBRA
1970	President ↓ Minister of Agriculture ↓ INCRA

for Colonization and Land Reform, INCRA, came as no surprise to disillusioned land reform advocates.[20]

Economic Development and National Integration

The post 1964 governments fixed their developmental goals on the attainment of sustained economic growth within a capitalist framework. This required, they decided, not just a reduction of the galloping inflation inherited from Goulart, but a reassessment of the import substitution experience of the fifties and early sixties. That experience, the economic architects of the post 1964 period claimed, resulted in imbalanced growth and distortions in the alloca- tion of resources as a consequence of inflation and price controls.[21] Through a series of developmental plans, including the Government's Economic Action Program, PAEG (1965), the Strategic Development Pro- gram, PED (1968/70), and the Economic and Social Development Plan, PND (1972/74), they proposed that Brazil achieve balanced growth in which the "expan- sion of markets depends on and adjusts itself to im- provement in productivity." The point was to avoid the strategy favored by CEPAL, through which a redis- tribution of income would "create markets without creating productivity and without concern for the future savings rate."[22] Besides bringing down infla- tion, these plans focussed on strengthening capital markets, instituting new credit mechanisms to increase the demand of investors, promote a redistribution of resources among regions and sectors by the use of tax incentives, and promote the growth and diversification of exports. Perhaps in part, as Baer notes, the con- tinuation of economic stagnation until 1968 can be attributed both to the immediate effects of the sta- bilization program and "the time-lag involved before the effects of the institutional reforms in the fi- nancial system could be felt and the numerous studies and plans for the expansion of the country's infra- structure and heavy industries could generate actual construction activities."[23] This period was followed,

however, by an extraordinary economic boom with a
real annual growth rate of ten percent.

One aspect of the military governments' development plans -- the reallocation of resources -- had
important implications, at least indirectly, for agriculture. Viewed as a corrollary to the agrarian
program being carried out by INCRA, it actually
served as a more faithful expression of recent agrarian policy than did the Land Statute. The National
Integration Program (PIN), brought into existence as
an aspect of the PND of 1972/74, proposed to integrate backward areas into the national mainstream
through programs of regional development. "In a
global sense, the purpose was to take advantage of
the most abundant means of production -- land and
labor -- in undertakings entailing low capital costs,
that is, in ranching and farming activities and public works, without interrupting the industrialization
process. This required a plan for the distribution
of land, colonization, and for infrastructure /devel-
opment/ in transportation.[24]

The PIN established a National Integration Fund
and the Program for Redistribution of Land and Sti-
mulus to Agroindustry in the North and Northeast,
PROTERRA, supported by thirty percent of the proceeds
of various sectoral and regional tax incentive programs (SUDENE -- Northeast, SUDAM -- Amazon region,
SUDEPE -- fishing, IBDF -- forestry, and EMBRATUR --
tourism). For the 1972/74 period, the two programs
were earmarked six billion cruzeiros (eight hundred
million dollars) for infrastructural development in
transportation; colonization along the full length of
the new thoroughfares (including the Transamazonic
and Cuiabá-Santarem highways); mineral exploration,

irrigation, and development of rail and river transportation corridors. PROTERRA would do for agriculture, it was planned, what the tax incentive program
of SUDENE had done for industry.[25] Northeast landowners with properties classified as latifundia were
faced with a carrot (tax relief) and stick (expropriation) approach as incentives to modernize their
properties and make them more productive. The effort
was viewed as a cooperative project between owners
and workers to remedy "defective" patterns of land
use and, on a voluntary basis, create small and medium rural enterprises." Clearly oriented toward the
middle income category rather than the poor, the plan
aimed to "eliminate the danger of merely consumer
(oriented) economies, that is, of family subsistence,
which do not at all represent individual progress or
collective development."[26] The larger the size of an
owner's total holdings, the greater the portion of
the land to be involved in the program: 20 percent
of 1,000 hectares; 30 percent of 1,001 to 3,000
hectares; 40 percent of 3,001 to 5,000 hectares, and
50 percent of over 5,000 hectares.[27] Under the supervision of designated financial institutions (Bank of
Brazil, Credito Fundiario, ABCAR), the owner was to
participate in planning the new developmental activity, contributing his knowledge of viable crops and
markets, and assisting in the definition of a work-
able land distribution program. The watchful eye of
PROTERRA and a "correct" policy of minimum prices
"will prevent this relationship between the small owner and the former latifundista from being established
to the detriment of the former."[28]

The Record of Reform

The meager evidence of land reform available after fifteen years of a new agrarian policy in Brazil affirms the overwhelming capitalist/developmental bias of the effort and the limited benefits yielded to the nation's poor. IBRA's initial goal had been to settle 200,000 camponeses a year on their own plots. By the end of 1966, IBRA's best period, it had succeeded in establishing only 4,000 families.[29] As of 1973, the total number of families newly established on their own property, including both expropriated and previously unoccupied land was 22,312, with over half the plots (12,408) distributed in the virgin territories of the northern states (Amazonas, Pará, Rondônia, Acre).[30]

In a review of the impact of ten years of agrarian reform policy on the Northeastern município of Caruaru in Pernambuco, a recent study noted that the problem of minifundia has grown rather than decreased and that tax, credit, and technical assistance policies have benefitted more prosperious owners. In the Northeast during the 1960/70 period, 90 percent of the increase in rural holdings occurred in the category of 10 hectares or less, with holdings of one hectare increasing most rapidly of all from 114,000 or 8 percent in 1960 to 350,000 or 16 percent in 1970. In 1960, 288,000 persons worked on these minifundia of under one hectare; in 1970, that figure had increased to 809,000 persons. Over the same ten year period, the 400,000 individuals working properties between one and two hectares in 1960 increased to over one million in 1970. In sum, approximately two million people, or a fourth of the region's agrarian work force, were working on properties of two hectares or less. Evidently, the eradication of minifundia and formation of a new rural middle class were not proceeding as rapidly as intended by the new agrarian policy and economic development plans.[31]

The existing rural middle and upper income categories, on the other hand, seemed well served by the new policies. Properties of one to two hectares were taxed at eight times the rate of those over fifty hectares, and a majority of credit applications were approved for properties over fifty hectares in size.[32] Finally, eligibility for tecynical assistance is limited to properties greater than ten hectares and, in practice, of the munícipio's 83 properties receiving assistance, the average size was 66.3 hectares.[33]

A major precept of those who equate economic development with capital intensive activities is that eventually traditional forms of land exploitation must give way not to a revamping of the land tenure structure, but to the consolidation of large commercial properties and the mechanization of agriculture.[34] Presumably, a policy discriminating against small proprietors should eventually maximize productivity by eliminating minifundia and encouraging urban migration of displaced individuals to find new employment opportunities in an expanding urban market.[35] In practice, however, this policy has resulted in an increase rather than a diminution of both minifundia and unemployment, especially in the Brazilian Northeast where the problem was gravest to begin with.

Moreover, this trend threatens more than just a persistance or increase in the number of rural poor. A recent study has pointed out that rather than caus-

ing "merely" or only humanitarian problems, a capital
intensive agrarian development policy "has direct and
important implications for increased productivity."[36]
It assumes a direct relationship between the profit
maximization of an individual firm and the economic
well being of the nation as a whole. "There is indeed an implicit assumption that somewhere policies
are being implimented to maintain full employment and
that when a laborer moves from one job to another it
always results in increased productivity. But these
are unwarranted assumptions in cases of less developed countries. Indeed, these assumptions point to
some of the critical problems of development."[37] In
a situation like that of Brazil, where income distribution is highly skewed, an increased volume of commodities does not automatically create greater consumer demand or generate sufficient jobs to absorb
displaced workers. Consequently, in the absence of a
labor intensive agrarian policy, even the recent res-
pectable growth in Brazilian agrarian productivity
(an average of 5.6 percent in real growth terms between 1968 and 1975)[38] does not immediately benefit
the rural poor, or, ultimately, serve the best interests of Brazilian national development.

THE MANAGEMENT OF CHANGE IN BRAZIL

This volume began by developing the thesis that
the Brazilian political system has maintained a high
degree of continuity with its patrimonial past. It
has remained authoritarian and dominated within its
statist framework by conservative elites. The democratic era of mobilizing populist politics between
1945 and 1964 was essentially anomalous and mislead-
ing in its illusive promises of sweeping reforms and
social benefits. Indeed, the fact that an agrarian

reform measure was ultimately enacted by a military regime in 1964 both affirmed the conservative pattern of Brazilian political development and served notice that incremental and conditional reformism, not populist revolution, would prevail as the dominant idiom of public policy. By the same token, intransigent latifundists who had joined the revolution to forestall any change were to find few allies among the influential industrial and commercial sectors and the developmentalists within the military regime.

The 1964 Land Statute thus capped a critical debate over the nature and pace of Brazilian development. In particular it posed the question of whether modernization of the rural sector would imply or necessitate a radical restructuring of Brazil's entire political and social order (perhaps on a Fidelista or Maoist scale); or whether it should be restricted to conservative economic measures relying on increased agricultural productivity to improve social conditions. Although the former contingency was always more hypothetical than real, the land reform issue nevertheless posed the alternatives of a mass mobilization system geared to redistributing wealth and property to the masses or of a traditional authoritarian order pursuing development within the existing corporatist, state capitalist framework.

The manner in which the 1964 crisis was resolved demonstrated that final decisions about Brazil's political future still rested with the corporatist elites and their underlying network of informal or tacit political controls. The formal "democratic" reconciliation system that functioned after World War II partially masked this reality and aggravated an important contradiction. On the one hand, the

corporatist elites were the real power brokers. On
the other, within the mechanisms of populist politics, they lacked direct formal means to influence
policy and control its implementation. When populism threatened the security of the corporatist establishment, upper class interests resorted to extra-
constitutional measures to bring about a deliberate
demobilization by severely limiting public access to
and participation in politics.

Viewed analytically, the apparent disruptions
of political regimes in Brazil should be regarded as
less a sign of chaos and lack of direction, than as
an historically established mode of coping with political crises threatening an undersirable redefinition of the political system. In their use of a
collective veto power over the fate of administrations and the course of development, the Brazilian
political elites, with the military at the head, have
reserved for themselves the right to establish the
rate and means by which new contenders could be incorporated into the political system and essential
conflicts over resources resolved. Such a pattern,
to be sure, is not uniquely Brazilian or, for that
matter, Latin American. Authoritarian rule has
often been regarded as necessary in managing high
rates of economic growth and social change. Planned
rapid transformations might otherwise be impossible
because of obstruction by specific traditional interests (such as latifundia owners) to such changes
on the one hand, or the intemperate demands for immediate redistribution of wealth by mass movements
on the other. Unfettered democracy under circumstances of rapid mobilization might overload the
political system with simultaneous demands and lead

to the destruction of corporatist influence and pri-
vilege.

Not surprisingly, to preserve their political
and economic hegemony,dominant interests preferred
that new social sectors enter into the Brazilian
political system not as autonomous actors in a representative democracy, but, more typically, as dependent subjects of a tutorial and paternalistic order.
This was true of the incorporation of the middle
class in 1930 and of the urban working class a few
years later in the course of the Vargas dictatorship.
These additions to the membership of accepted participants in the political process reordered the relative importance of various groups within the corporatist establishment. As the focus of economic activity shifted from agriculture to industry, the corporatist leadership expanded to include new industrial
and professional groups. These newcomers then began
to eclipse the agrarian sector. But these changes,
reflections of the pressures created by economic
modernization for social and political integration,
have thus far reaffirmed the continued validity and
vitality of an institutional framework firmly rooted
in a patrimonial past. To be sure, in safeguarding
these institutions, the supporters of the Brazilian
authoritarian state have not merely conformed to a
preordained fate. The political and economic events
of Brazilian history are also the reflection of developmental priorities and deliberate choices made
by an elite determined to insure the continuity of
the traditional political order and therefore of its
own supremacy.

Given the improbability of a revolutionary redirection of the Brazilian developmental strategy,

it would seem that a pragmatic incremental approach offers the most hope for reform. Historically, Brazil has demonstrated that it favors a style of decision making that is open ended and based on coalition building. An awareness of the flexibility of the Brazilian system must also, however, be combined with an understanding of the present leadership's priorities in order to be able to speculate about the future. On that score, it is clear that the primary objectives of the military government are the generation of wealth, economic growth, and an international status ultimately equivalent to that of the first ranking world powers. The present Brazilian leadership is in no sense willing to risk dreams of greatness (the saying goes, "God is a Brazilian") for a gamble on social reforms, the direct benefits of which may take time to materialize.

However, the military and their supporters must understand that ignoring pressures for greater economic equity and political participation by the lower classes, and particularly the rural masses, is also risky. Rural unrest in Brazil has not been abolished; it has only been contained. The social and economic conditions and political pressures that produced it in the first place have persisted and in some instances been aggravated. Ultimately, the degree of Brazil's greatness and international prominence, not to speak of the state's moral and ethical legitimacy, will depend on the creation of an institutional structure capable of absorbing changes without resorting to costly disruptions and repression. The optimal use of all its rich resources requires, in the final analysis, that Brazil devise a developmental strategy premised not on the marginalization exploitation of a large part of its population, but in harnessing the useful and willing energies of the entire nation. The ability of the Brazilian conservative leadership to make choices insuring this outcome depends to a considerable degree on their acknowledging that in the long run their security and well being are better served by incorporating the economic costs of social equity and political humanism into developmental goals than by prolonging policies of costly political repression.

NOTES

1. As Barraclough and Domike observed in an overview of Latin American land reform activity in the early sixties, choices within a given framework are possible, "but the institutional and political limits on policy alternatives are much narrower than perceived by outside observers." "Agrarian Structure in Seven Latin American Countries." p. 392.

2. In interviews, officers of industrial and commercial associations could see little, if any, relation between agrarian issues and problems and their own interests. Landowners, conversely, complained that they were routinely ignored and misunderstood both by other groups and the government.

3. Op. cit.

4. E.M. Schattschneider, The Semi-Sovereign People. A Realist's View of Democracy in America (Hillsdale, Ill.: The Dryden Press, 1960), pp. 7-8.

5. Journeys Toward Progress.

6. IBRA was established as an autarchy by Decree Law No. 55,889 of March 31, 1965. Campanhôle, Legislação Agrária, p. 194.

7. The questionnaires for the survey were distributed to landowners by the mayor of each municipio. The largest owners tended to ignore the survey both because of its potential threat to their status and also because they could dismiss the possible threat of a fine for noncompliance as unimportant. The most delinquent states were São Paulo, Rio de Janeiro, and Guanabara. Conferência, 1966, p. 17; and interviews with IBRA officials.

8. The survey disclosed, for example, that there were 1,000 more land holdings in Brazil than had been reported by the 1960 census. Also, a number of land owners discovered for the first time the actual dimensions of their property.

9. Conferência, 1966, pp. 4, 5.

10. The full text of the Land Statute, Decree Law 4,504 of November 30, 1964 is reproduced in Campanhole, Legislação Agrária.

11. Doreen Warriner, Land Reform in Principle and Practice (London: Clarendon Press, 1969) p. 292.

12. Osny Duarte Pereira, "O Estatuto de Reforma Agrária," Revista Civilização Brasileira 1, 1965, p. 25. See also IBRA, O ITR Calculado (Rio de Janeiro: IBRA, 1966).

13. Interest Politics in Brazil, p. 255.

14. Initially, priority areas were decreed in the states of Minas Gerais, Rio de Janeiro, Rio Grande do Sul, Pernambuco. These states had experienced some of the highest incidences of rural violence.

15. Much of IBRA's energy in the first months went into analyzing and explaining to others this complicated taxation system. See for example, O ITR Calculado.

16. William R. Cline, Economic Consequences of a Land Reform in Brazil (London: North Holland Publishing Company, 1970) p. 167. Cline's study is largely theoretical and reviews the law and its hypothetical rather than actual impact. Hirschman provides a more spirited discussion of alternative agrarian strategies in Journeys Toward Progress, chapter 2, "Land Use and Land Reform in Colombia," pp. 134-213.

17. Ibid., pp. 183, 184.

18. Ibid., pp. 184, 187.

19. JB, May 20, 1969 contains the text of this decree.

20. Decree Law No. 1110, July 9, 1970.

21. Werner Baer, "The Brazilian Growth and Development Experience: 1964 - 1975" in Riordan Roett, editor, Brazil in the Seventies (Washington, D. C.: American Enterprise Institute for Public Policy Research, 1976), p. 43.

22. Victor da Silva and Mircea Buescu, Dez Anos de Renovação Econômica (Rio de Janeiro: APEC, 1974), p. 39. Also see pp. 23-47 for a discussion of the objectives of the three development plans.

23. "The Brazilian Growth and Development Experience," p. 46.

24. Silva and Buescu, p. 98.

25. Ibid., pp. 98, 99.

26. Arthur Pio dos Santos, "PROTERRA, Reforma Agrária Consentida," Revista do Directo Agrário 1 (1973), p. 14.

27. Ibid., p. 13.

28. Ibid., p. 15.

29. Conferência, 1966, p. 17.

30. Instituto Nacional de Colonização e Reforma Agrária, Relatório Anual, 1973 (Ministerio de Agricultura, 1973), pp. 33-35.

31. Douglas Young and Kenton Corum, "Impacto da Políticas Agrárias no Tamanho das Propriedades. Um Estudo no Município de Caruaru no Agreste de Pernambuco," Boletim Econômico, 3, 1975, pp. 21, 22.

32. Ibid., p. 25.

33. Ibid., p. 27.

34. For an extensive discussion of agricultural development in Brazil using this approach, see G. Edward Schuh, The Agricultural Development of Brazil (New York: Praeger, 1970). Two Brazilian sources which provide comprehensive discussions from this perspective are IPES, A Reforma Agrária, and Ben Hur Raposo, A Reforma Agrária para o Brasil (Rio de Janeiro: Fundo de Cultura, 1965). Raposo worked for the landowners' confederation at the time the book was written.

35. Young and Corum, p. 27.

36. Peter Dorner, "Needed Redirection in Economic Analysis," in Peter Dorner, editor, Land Reform in Latin America: Issues and Cases (Madison, Wisconsin: Land Economics, 1971), p. 11.

37. Ibid., p. 15.

38. Baer, p. 47.

Appendix: Note on Sources

As noted in the Preface, interviews for this study were
conducted with a promise of confidentiality and anonymity, and
are therefore not listed. It is possible, however, to indicate
the scope and range of the interviews I conducted.

I interviewed sixty-eight individuals between January and
October 1969, several of them more than once. To obtain as
broad and complete a picture as possible of political and social
group participation in the agrarian issue, I interviewed minister of state, administrators, senators, federal deputies, and
political party leaders associated with both the Goulart and
the Castelo Branco governments. I also conducted interviews
with officials and members of the national confederations of
agriculture, industry, and commerce, and with those of state
federations in São Paulo, Guanabara, and Rio Grande do Sul.
Finally, my interviews included discussions with leaders in
agricultural workers' syndicates, with representatives of the
Catholic church, and with military officers.

CONTENT ANALYSIS OF THE AGRARIAN DEBATE
IN THE CHAMBER OF DEPUTIES

The universe consisted of 189 deputies who participated in
the congressional debate on land reform for the three year
period of 1962-1964. The content of every deputy's speeches and

remarks on the agrarian issue was scanned for attitudinal information and classified according to the code which follows. Ordinal ranking was used for items 2 and 5-9. The primary purpose of the analysis was to obtain an aggregate view of particular attitudinal characteristics, and in certain instances measures of association (Gamma and Lambda) between key attitudes.

Code

1. State which the deputy represents.

2. Political party affiliation.

3. Number of times the deputy spoke on agrarian issue in 1962, 1963, 1964.

4. Introduced agrarian legislation (n.a., no, yes).

5. Perception of issue; evaluation of problem (n.a., no, yes):

    a. problem exists

    b. problem is economic

    c. problem is social

    d. problem is cultural

    e. problem is nation-wide

    f. problem is regional

    g. problem is a communist plot

    h. problem is artificially created by politicians to gain power.

6. Attitude toward specific measures (n.a., no, yes):

    a. favors credit programs

    b. favors extension services

    c. favors colonization programs

    d. favors progressive taxation

    e. favors forced leasing of land

    f. favors expropriation of idle land payable in cash

    g. favors expropriation of idle land payable in bonds

7. Attitude toward amending constitution (n.a., no, yes):

    a. in principle against any change

    b. against any changes affecting property

c. for, if for good social reason

d. for, if "the people demand it"

8. Political orientation to land reform issue (n.a., no, yes):

a. land reform necessary regardless of political circumstances

b. land reform undesirable, regardless of political circumstances

c. land reform is as desirable as the government in power at the time

d. President Goulart can be trusted with a constitutional amendment and land reform law

e. President Castelo Branco can be trusted with a constitutional amendment and land reform law

9. Reaction to specific legislative measures (n.a., against, for):

a. Brizola bill

b. Goulart-PTB amendment proposal and land bill

c. PSD-PTB compromise

d. Milton Campos bill

e. Badra bill

f. Estatuto da Terra

Glossary of Brazilian Terms and Acronyms

bossa nova: left wing of the UDN

bachareis: liberal intellectuals (identified with the UDN)

camponês: farmer, peasant, agricultural worker, countryman

carioca: native of the city of Rio de Janeiro

CNA: National Confederation of Agriculture (before 1966, the CRB)

compactos: radical wing of the PTB

coronel: rural political boss

CRB: Brazilian Rural Confederation (in 1966 became the CNA)

Estado Nôvo: literally "New State," a neofascist regime established by Getúlio Vargas 1937-45.

fazendeiro: land owner, usually understood to be a large property owner

gaucho: native of the state of Rio Grande do Sul

IBAD: Brazilian Institute for Democratic Action (private pressure group)

IBRA: Brazilian Agrarian Reform Institute

INCRA: National Institute of Colonization and Agrarian Reform

INDA: Brazilian Agrarian Development Institute

IPES: Institute for Social Research and Studies (private pressure group)

ligas camponesas: "peasant" leagues (see camponês, above) established by Francisco Julião.

mineiro: native of the state of Minas Gerais

município: local government unit below state level, roughly comparable to a municipal district.

paulista: native of the state of São Paulo

pelego: literally, sheepskin placed under a saddle. Colloquially used for more or less covert government agent or
lackey in labor union.

pessedista: member of the PSD

petebista: member of the PTB

poder moderador: moderating, or mediating power of the emperor.

PSD: Social Democratic Party

PTB: Brazilian Labor Party

SUDENE: Superintendency for the Development of the Northeast

SUPRA: Superintendency for Agrarian Reform

udenista: member of the UDN

UDN: National Democratic Union

Bibliography

BRAZILIAN PUBLIC DOCUMENTS

Câmara dos Deputados. Anais da Câmara dos Deputados. Rio de
    Janeiro: Congresso Nacional, 1962-1964.

Congresso Nacional. Diario do Congresso Nacional. Rio de
    Janeiro: Congresso Nacional, 1962-1964.

Decreto n. 74,794 de 29 out. 74. Programa de Desenvolvimento
    de Areas Integradas do Nordeste. POLONORDESTE. Expo-
    sição de Motivos Interministerial n. 269-B, de 29 de
    outubro de 1974.

Instituto Brasileiro de Geografia e Estatística. Anuário
    Estatístico do Brasil. Rio de Janeiro: lBGE, 1954-1964.

_____. Projeto do II Plano Nacional de Desenvolvimento, PND,
    1975-1979. Rio de Janeiro: lBGE, 1974.

_____. Sinopse Estatística do Brasil, 1975. Rio de Janeiro:
    lBGE, 1975.

Instituto Brasileiro de Reforma Agrária. As Areas Priori-
    tárias. Decretos. Rio de Janeiro: IBRA, n.d.

_____. Encôntro Sobre Ocupação do Territorio. Rio de
    Janeiro: IBRA, 1967.

_____. Estrutura Agrária Brasileira. Rio de Janeiro,
    IBRA, 1967.

_____. O ITR Calculado. Rio de Janeiro: IBRA, 1966.

_____. Regulamento Geral. Decreto No. 55.889 de 31 de
    marco de 1965. Rio de Janeiro: IBRA, 1965.

_____. "Síntese das Principais Realizações, 1967/1968."
Typescript.

Instituto Brasileiro de Reforma Agrária Regional/Rio Grande do
Sul. Realidade Agrária do Rio Grande do Sul. Pôrto
Alegre: IBRAR/RS, 1969.

Ministerio de Agricultura. Instituto Nacional de Colonização
e Reforma Agrária. Relatório Anual, 1973. Rio de
Janeiro: INCRA, 1973.

_____. Instituto Nacional de Desenvolvimento Agrário.
Estatuto da Terra. Lei N. 4.504 de 30 de Novembro de
1964. Departamento de Imprenta Nacional, 1965.

Ministério de Planejamento e Coordenação Econômica. Programa
de Ação Econômica do Govêrno, 1964-1966. Rio de Janeiro:
Civilização Brasileira, 1972.

Monteiro Filho, Armando. Anteprojeto de Reforma Agrária. Rio
de Janeiro: Ministério de Agricultura, Serviço de In-
formação Agrícola, 1962.

Senado. Anais do Senado. Rio de Janeiro: Congresso Nacional,
1962-1964.

NEWSPAPERS AND JOURNALS CONSULTED

Correio da Manhã (CM), 1962-1965.

Estado de São Paulo, select issues.

Folha de São Paulo, select issues.

Gleba, 1958-1969.

Jornal do Brasil (JB), 1961-1964.

Jornal do Comércio, select issues.

Tribuna da Imprensa, select issues.

Visão, 1961-1966.

UNPUBLISHED SOURCES

Borges, Thomas Pompeu de Accioly. "Novos Rumos para a Reforma

Agrária Brasileira." Internal document of the Grupo de
Trabalho sobre Reforma Agrária. Rio de Janeiro, 1968.
Typescript.

_____. "O Estatuto da Terra." Perguntas Formuladas por T.
Pompeu Accioly Borges ao Dr. Paulo Assis Ribeiro, Presi-
dente do IBRA, por Ocasião de sua Conferência no Club de
Engenharia, o Dia 12 de Maio de 1966. Mimeographed.

Britto, Flavio da Costa. Relatório das Atividades da Confederação Nacional de Agricultura em 1968. Brasília, D.F.
1969. Mimeographed.

Cavalcanti, Amaro. "Cadastro Rural e Crédito Agrícola."
Recife: Centro Sulamericano de Credito Agrícola, 1958.
Mimeographed.

Confederação Nacional de Agricultura. "A Agricultura Brasileira." Mimeographed, 1969.

Confederação Rural Brasileira. Relatório das Atividades em
1965. Rio de Janeiro, 1965. Mimeographed.

_____. "Sindicalização Rural." Rio de Janeiro, n.d. Mimeo-
graphed.

Federação dos Trabalhadores na Agricultura Gauchos. Carta de
Reivindicações do IV Congresso Estadual. Pôrto Alegre,
12 a 14 de Julho de 1969. Mimeographed.

_____. "O Clero e a Frente Agrária Gaucha." Pôrto Alegre,
n.d. Mimeographed.

Lamounier, Bolivar. "Ideology and Authoritarian Regimes:
Theoretical Perspectives and a Study of the Brazilian
Case." Ph.D. dissertation, UCLA, 1974.

Leite, Edgar Teixeira. "Direito Agrário e Justiça Rural na
Renovação Agrícola do Brasil." Conferência pronunciada
no Instituto dos Advogados do Brasil. Rio de Janeiro,
1969. Mimeographed.

_____. "Reforma Agrária. Destinação Econômica e Social da
Terra." Observações sobre o Anteprojeto da Comissão
Especial. Rio de Janeiro: Conselho Nacional de Economia,
n.d. Mimeographed.

Menges, Constantine. "The Politics of Agrarian Reform in
Chile." Ph.D. dissertation. Columbia University, 1969.

Meinberg, Iris. "Plano de Trabalho (1967--1968--1969)

Apresentado pelo Presidente Iris Meinberg ao Conselho de Representantes." Rio de Janeiro: CNA, 1967. Mimeographed.

Peterson, Phyllis Jane. "Brazilian Political Parties: Formation, Organization and Leadership, 1945-1959." Ph.D. dissertation, University of Michigan, 1962.

Ribeiro, Paulo Assis. Conferência no Conselho Nacional de Economia. Rio de Janeiro, 1966. Mimeographed.

_____. "Implantação da Reforma Agrária." Relatório de Abril 1964--Março 1967. Rio de Janeiro, 1967. Mimeographed.

Schilling, Arno. "Sindicalização Rural." Pôrto Alegre, 1969. Mimeographed.

Wilkie, Mary E. "A Report on the Rural Syndicates in Pernambuco." Rio de Janeiro: Centro de Pesquisas em Ciências Sociais, 1964. Mimeographed.

OTHER WORKS

Alexander, Robert J. "Nature and Progress of Agrarian Reform in Latin America." Journal of Economic History, No. 23 (December 1963). Pp. 559-73.

Alvarenza, Octavio Mello. "Justiça Agrária, Considerações Estruturais, Face a Realidade Brasileira." Revista do Direito Agrário 1(1973): 47--51.

Andrade, Manuel Correia de. A Terra e o Homem no Nordeste. São Paulo: Editôra Brasiliense, 1963.

Baer, Werner. Industrialization and Economic Development in Brazil. Homewood, Ill.: 1965.

Baklanoff, Eric N., ed. New Perspectives of Brazil. Nashville: Vanderbilt University Press, 1966.

Barraclough, Solon L. and Domike, Arthur L. "Agrarian Structures in Seven Latin American Countries." Land Economics 42(1966): 391-424.

Barros, Enrique de. A Estrutura Agrária como Obstáculo a Ação Agronômica. A Reforma Agrária como Problema Econômico. São Paulo: Escola de Sociologia e Política de São Paulo, 1954.

Beltrão, Hélio. A Revolução e o Desenvolvimento. Aula inaugural dos cursos da Escola Superior de Guerra. Rio

242

de Janeiro: IBGE, 1969.

Borba, Lauro.   Organização da Vida Rural.   Recife: Federação das Associações Rurais do Estado de Pernambuco, 1952.

Callado, Antônio.   Os Industriais da Seca e os "Galileus" de Pernambuco.   Riode Janeiro: Civilização Brasileira, 1960.

Campanhôle, Adriano, ed., Consolidação das Leis do Trabalho e Legislação Complementar.   São Paulo: Editôra Atlas,1966.

Campanhôle, Adriano, ed., Legislação Agrária.   São Paulo: Atlas, 1969.

Campanhôle, Adriano, and Campanhole, Hilton Lôbo.   Legislação Agrária.   6th ed.   São Paulo: Editora Atlas, 1974.

Campos, Roberto de Oliveira.   Política Econômica e Mitos Políticos.   Rio de Janeiro: APEC, 1965.

Cardoso, Fernando Henrique.   Autoritarismo e Democratização.   Rio de Janeiro: Paz e Terra, 1975.

_____.   "Tensões Sociais no Campo e Reforma Agrária."   Revista Brasileira de Estudos Políticos.   N. 12 (outubro 1961).   Pp. 7-26.

Cehelsky, Marta.   "A Case Study in Urbanization: Brazil."   Population and Urbanization Problems of Latin America.   Edited by Philip B. Taylor and Sam Schulman.   Houston: University of Houston, 1971.

_____.   "Redistributive Policy and Agrarian Reform."   Contemporary Brazil: Issues in Economic and Political Development.   Edited by H. Jon Rosenbaum and William G. Tyler.   New York: Praeger, 1972.

Cesarino Júnior, A.F.   "Conceito de Trabalhador Rural para Efeito de Enquadramento Sindical."   Jurídica, No. 100 (janeiro--março, 1968).

Cline, William R.   Economic Consequences of a Land Reform in Brazil.   London: North-Holland Publishing Company, 1970.

Comité Interamericano sobre Desarrollo Agrário.   Land Tenure Conditions and Socio-Economic Development in Brazil.   Washington, D.C.:   Pan American Union, 1963.

Confederação Nacional de Agricultura. Novas Sugestões ao Govêrno da República.   Serie Problemas Gerais.   Riode Janeiro:

Irmãos Di Giorgio, 1967.

_____. Sistema Tributário Nacional: Lei No. 5.172 de 25/10/ 66. Rio de Janeiro: CNA, n.d.

_____. Confederação Nacional dos Trabalhadores na Agricultura. Diretrizes das Classes Patronais e Trabalhadoras. Rio de Janeiro, 1969.

Confederação Rural Brasileira. "A Agricultura Brasileira. Diretrizes para um Plano de Ação." Memorial da CRB ao Exmo. Senhor Presidente da Republica, Doutor Jânio da Silva Quadros. Gleba, (Março 1961).

_____. Política Rural. Rio de Janeiro, 1968.

_____. "Quarta Conferência Rural." Rio de Janeiro: Gleba, 1962.

_____. (Confederação Nacional de Agricultura). Sindicalização Rural. Rio de Janeiro: CRB, n.d.

Corbisier, Roland. Reforma ou Revolução? Rio de Janeiro: Civilização Brasileira, 1968.

Cunha, Euclides da. Rebellion in the Backlands. Chicago: University of Chicago Press, 1944.

Da Silva, José Gomes. A Reforma Agrária no Brasil. Rio de Janeiro: Zahar Editores, 1971.

Dean, Warren Kempton. The Industrialization of Sao Paulo, 1880-1945. Austin: The University of Texas Press, 1969.

_____. "The Problem of the Latifundia in Nineteenth Century Brazil." Hispanic American Historical Review, (November, 1971).

Delfim Neto, Antônio. "Agricultura e Desenvolvimento." Mundo Econômico 10, (1967).

Diegues Júnior, Manuel. População e Açucar no Nordeste do Brasil. Rio de Janeiro: Comissão Nacional de Alimentação, 1965.

_____. População e Propriedade da Terra no Brasil. Washington, D.C.: Pan American Union, 1959.

Dorner, Peter, ed. Land Reform in Latin America: Issues and Cases. Madison, Wisconsin: Land Economics, 1971.

Dulles, John W.F. Vargas of Brazil: A Political Biography. Austin: The University of Texas Press, 1967.

Dutra, Eloy. IBAD, Sigla da Corrupção. Rio de Janeiro: Civilização Brasileira, 1963.

Eisenstadt, S.M. The Political Systems of Empires. New York: The Free Press, 1969.

Ellis, Howard S. The Economy of Brazil. Berkeley: University of California Press, 1969.

Erickson, Kenneth P. The Brazilian Corporative State and Working Class Politics. Berkeley, University of California Press, 1977.

_____. "Corporatism and Labor in Development." Contemporary Brazil: Issues in Economic and Political Development. Edited by H. Jon Rosenbaum and William G. Tyler. New York: Praeger, 1972.

Faoro, Raymundo. Os Donos do Poder. Pôrto Alegre: Editorial Globo, 1958.

Feder, Ernst. The Rape of the Peasantry. New York: Doubleday, 1971.

Federação dos Trabalhadores na Agricultura no Rio Grande do Sul. FETAG. História/Trabalho/Preocupações. Pôrto Alegre, 1969.

Federação dos Trabalhadores na Agricultura Gauchos. Relatôrio. Pôrto Alegre: FETAG, 1968.

Fiechter, Georges-Andre. Brazil Since 1964: Modernization Under a Military Regime. New York: John Wiley, 1975.

Frente Agrária Gaucha. Verdade e Justiça para o Homem do Campo. Pôrto Alegre, n.d.

Freyre, Gilberto. Ordem e Progresso. Rio de Janeiro: Editôra José Olympio, 1959.

Furtado, Celso. Análise do Modelo Brasileiro. Rio de Janeiro: Civilização Brasileira, 1972.

_____. The Economic Growth of Brazil. Translated by Ricardo W. de Aguiar and Eric Charles Drysdale. Berkeley: University of California Press, 1965.

Galjert, Benno. "Class and 'Following' in Rural Brazil."

245

América Latina 7 (1964): 3-24.

Geisel, Ernesto. "O Homem e o Campo." Planejamento e Desenvolvimento 4(1976): 26-31.

Graham, Richard. "Landowners and the Overthrow of the Empire."
Luso-Brazilian Review 7 (1970): 44-56.

Guimarães, Alberto Passos. Quatro Séculos de Latifúndio. Rio
de Janeiro: Pax e Terra, 1968.

Hirschman, Albert O. Journeys Toward Progress. New York:
Doubleday, 1965.

Horowitz, Irving Louis. Revolution in Brazil. New York:
Dutton, 1964.

Huizer, Gerrit. "Some Notes on Community Development and Social Research." América Latina, 8 (1965): 128-44.

Huntington, Samuel. Political Order in Changing Societies.
New Haven: Yale University Press, 1968.

_____, and Moore, Clement H. Authoritarian Politics in
Modern Society. New York: Basic Books, 1970.

Ianni, Octavio. O Colapso do Populismo no Brasil. Rio de
Janeiro: Civilização Brasileira, 1968.

_____. "A Constituição do Proletariado Agrícola no Brasil."
Revista Brasileira de Estudos Políticos 12 (1961): 27-46.

_____. Estado e Capitalismo. Rio de Janeiro: Civilização
Brasileiro, 1965.

_____, et al. Política e Revolução Social no Brasil. Rio de
Janeiro: Civilização Brasileira, 1964.

Institute for the Comparative Study of Political Systems.
Edited by Ronald Schneider, Charles Daugherty, and James
Rowe. Brazil Election Factbook. Washington, D.C.:
Operations and Policy Research, 1965.

Instituto Brasileiro de Ação Democrática. Recomendações sobre
Reforma Agrária. Rio de Janeiro: IBAD, 1961.

Instituto de Ciências Socias. Bibliografia sobre Reforma
Agrária. Rio de Janeiro: Universidade do Brasil, 1962.

Instituto de Pesquisas e Estudos Sociais. A Reforma Agrária:
Problemas, Bases, e Soluções. Rio de Janeiro: IPES, 1964.

Ionescu, Ghita, and Gellner, Ernest, eds. Populism, its Meanings and National Characteristics. London: Weidenfeld and Nicolson, 1969.

Jaguaribe, Helio. "A Crise Brasileira." Cadernos de Nosso Tempo 1 (1953): 120-60.

_____. Economic and Political Development. Translated by Suzette Macedo. Cambridge, Massachusetts: Harvard University Press, 1968.

Julião, Francisco, ed. Ligas Camponesas: Outubro 1962-Abril 1964. Cuernavaca: CIDOC, 1969.

Kaufman, Robert. The Chilean Political Right and Agrarian Reform. Resistance and Moderation. Washington, D.C.: ICOPS, 1967.

_____. The Politics of Land Reform in Chile, 1950-1970. Public Policy, Political Institutions, and Social Change. Cambridge, Mass.: Harvard University Press, 1972.

Keller, Suzanne. Beyond the Ruling Class. New York: Random House, 1964.

Landsberger, Henry, A., ed. Latin American Peasant Movements. Ithaca, N.Y.: Cornell University Press, 1969.

Lapalombara, Joseph. "The Utility and Limitations of Interest Group Theory in Non-American Field Situations." Journal of Politics, XXII (February, 1960).

Leal, Victor Nunes. Coronelismo, Enxada e Voto. Rio de Janeiro: Livraria Forense, 1949.

Leeds, Anthony. "Brazilian Careers and Social Structure: An Evolutionary Model and Case History." American Anthropologist 66, Part I (1964): 1321-47.

Leite, Edgar Teixeira. "Aspectos do Complexo Agrário Brasileiro." Carta Mensal do Conselho Técnico da Confederação Nacional da Industria 180 (1970).

_____. "Aspectos da Sindicalização Rural no Brasil." Jurídica, XXXI (abril-junho, 1966).

_____. "O Problema da Terra no Brasil." Revista Brasileira de Geografia. (abril-junho, 1959).

_____. A Revolução Agrícola pela Tecnificação do Homem Rural. Rio de Janeiro: Confederação Nacional de Agricultura, 1967.

247

Leff, Nathaniel. Economic Policy-Making and Development in Brazil, 1947-1964. New York: Wiley, 1968.

Levine, Robert M. The Vargas Regime: The Critical Years, 1934-1938. New York: Columbia University Press, 1970.

Linz, Juan. "An Authoritarian Regime: Spain." In Cleavages, Ideologies and Party Systems. Edited by Erik Allardt and Yrjo Littune. Helsinki, 1964.

Lopes, Juarez R.B. A Crise do Brasil Arcáico. São Paulo: Difusão Européia do Livro, 1967.

_____. Desenvolvimento e Mudança Social. São Paulo: Companhia Editôra Nacional, 1968.

Love, Joseph L. Rio Grande do Sul and Brazilian Regionalism, 1882-1930. Stanford, California: Stanford University Press, 1971.

Lowi, Theodore. "American Business, Public Policy, Case Studies, and Political Theory." World Politics, 4(1964).

Ludwig, Armin D., and Taylor, Harry W. Brazil's New Agrarian Reform. An Evaluation of its Property Classification and Tax Systems. New York: Praeger, 1969.

Maia, J. Motta. "O Estatuto da Terra. Apreciação e Texto." Jurídica 29(1964).

Marcondes, J.V. Freitas. "O Sindicalismo Rural e a Reforma Agrária." Revista Brasileira de Estudos Políticos 20(1966): 49-58.

Martins, José de Sousa. A Imigração e a Crise do Brasil Agrário. São Paulo: Editôra Pioneira, 1973.

Meinberg, Iris. "São Empresarios o Pequeno Proprietário, O Arrendatário e o Parceiro." Gleba 13(1967).

Moore, Barrington. The Social Origins of Dictatorship and Democracy. Lord and Peasant in the Making of the Modern World. Boston: Beacon Press, 1966.

Pedreira, Fernando. Março 31. Civis e Militares no Processo da Crise Brasileira. Rio de Janeiro: José Alvaro, 1964.

Pereira, Osny Duarte. A Constituição Federal e Suas Modifica-ções Incorporadas ao Texto. Rio de Janeiro; Civiliza-ção Brasileira, 1966.

_____. "O Estatuto de Reforma Agrária." Revista Civiliza-
ção Brasileira 1(1965): 24-44.

Petras, James F. and La Porte Jr., Robert. Cultivating Revolution. The United States and Agrarian Reform. New York:
Random House, 1971.

Prado Jr., Caio. "Contribuição para a Análise da Questão
Agrária no Brasil." Revista Brasiliense 28(1960):
165-238.

_____. "O Estatuto do Trabalhador Rural." Revista Brasil--
iense 47(1963): 1-13.

_____. História Econômica do Brasil. 11th edition. São
Paulo: Editôra Brasiliense, 1969.

Puggina, Adolpho. Reforma Agrária. A Reforma das Reformas.
Pôrto Alegre: FETAG, 1968.

Raposo, Ben Hur. A Reforma Agrária para o Brasil. Rio de
Janeiro: Fundo de Cultura, 1965.

Ribeiro, Paulo de Assis. Conferência Realizada no Conselho
Nacional de Economia. Rio de Janeiro: IBRA, 1966.

Rodriguez, Dom Orlando, et al. Declaração do Morro Alto. Programa de Política Agrária Conforme os Princípios de Reforma Agrária, Questão de Consciência. São Paulo:
Editôra Vera Cruz, 1964.

_____. Reforma Agrária, Questão de Consciência. São Paulo:
Editôra Vera Cruz, 1960.

Roett, Riordan, editor. Brazil in the Seventies. Washington,
D.C.: American Enterprise Institute for Public Policy
Research, 1976,

_____, editor. Brazil in the Sixties. Nashville, Tenn.:
Vanderbilt University Press, 1972.

Rokeach, Milton. Beliefs, Attitudes, and Values. San
Francisco: Jossey-Bass, 1969.

Rustow, Dankwart A. A World of Nations. Washington, D.C.:
The Brookings Institution, 1967.

Sampaio, Pericles. "Previdência Rural: Linhas Gerais, Aspectos Jurídicos." Revista Brasileira de Estudos Políticos
35(1973): 69-79.

249

Santos, Arthur Pio dos. "PROTERRA: Reforma Agrária Consentida." Revista do Direito Agrário 1(1973): 9-12.

Schattschneider, E.E. The Semi-Sovereign People. A Realist's View of Democracy in America. New York: Holt, Rinehart, and Winston, 1960.

Scherer, Cardeal D. Vicente. A Questão Agrária. Pôrto Alegre, n.d.

Schmitter, Philippe C. Interest Conflict and Political Change in Brazil. Stanford, California: Stanford University Press, 1971.

Schneider, Ronald M. Brazil. Foreign Policy of a Future World Power. Boulder, Colorado: Westview Press, 1976.

_____. The Political System of Brazil. Emergence of a "Modernizing" Authoritarian Regime. New York: Columbia University Press, 1971.

Schuh, G. Edward, in collaboration with Eliseu Roberto Alves. The Agricultural Development of Brazil. New York: Praeger, 1970.

Siekman, Philip. "When Executives Turned Revolutionaries." Fortune, September, 1964.

Silva, José Gomes da. A Reforma Agrária no Brasil. Frustração Camponesa ou Instrumento de Desenvolvimento. Rio de Janeiro: Zahar Editores, 1971.

Silva, Victor da, and Buescu, Mircea. Dez Anos de Renovação Econômica. Rio de Janeiro: APEC, 1974.

Simonsen, Mario Henrique. A Nova Economia Brasileira. Rio de Janeiro: Livraria José Olympio, 1974.

Singer, Paulo. Desenvolvimento Econômico e Evolução Urbana. São Paulo: Universidade de São Paulo, 1968.

Skidmore, Thomas E. Politics in Brazil, 1930-1964. New York: Oxford University Press, 1967.

Smith, T. Lynn, editor. Agrarian Reform in Latin America. New York: Alfred A Knopf, 1965.

Stavenhagen, Rodolfo, editor. Agrarian Problems and Peasant Movements in Latin America. New York: Doubleday, 1970.

Stein, Stanley. Vassouras, A Brazilian Coffee County, 1850-1900. Cambridge, Massachusetts: Harvard University Press, 1957.

Stepan, Alfred, editor. Authoritarian Brazil: Origins, Policies, and Future. New Haven: Yale University Press, 1973.

_____. The Military in Politics. Changing Patterns in Brazil. Princeton, New Jersey: Princeton University Press, 1971.

Tavares, Assis. "Caio Prado e a Teoria da Revolução Brasileira." Revista Civilização Brasileira 11-12(1967): 48-80.

Torres, João Camilo de Oliveira. A Democrácia Coroada. Rio de Janeiro: Livraria José Olympio, 1957.

_____. Estratificação Social no Brasil. São Paulo: Difusão Européia do Livro, 1965.

Veliz, Claudio, editor. Obstacles to Change in Latin America. New York: Oxford University Press, 1965.

Vera, Nestor. "O Congresso Camponês em Belo Horizonte." Revista Brasiliense. 39(1962): 499.

Viana Filho, Luis. O Govêrno Castelo Branco. Rio de Janeiro: Livraria José Olympio, 1975.

Vinhas, M. Problemas Agrario-Camponeses dc Brasil. Rio de Janeiro: Civilização Brasileira, 1968.

Warriner, Doreen. Land Reform in Principle and Practice. London: Clarendon Press, 1969.

Wirth, John. The Politics of Brazilian Development, 1930-1954. Stanford, California: Stanford University Press, 1970.

Young, Douglas, and Corum, Kenton. "Impacto das Políticas Agrárias no Tamanho das Propriedades. Um Estudo no Município de Caruaru no Nordeste de Pernambuco." Boletim Econômico 3(1975): 21-33.

Index

PSD-mineiro proposal,
143, 145-146
ARENA, See National Renovation
Alliance
Armed forces, See Military
Arrais, Miguel, 103
Authoritarian rule, 15, 22
225-230
and agrarian issue, 34, 226
Cartorial State and, 24-25
changes of regime in, 15-17
Congress and, 119, 161
patrimonialism and, 16-21
80-86, 225
populism as an aspect of,
30, 77
theories of, 4-5
See also Corporatism;
Military

Badra, Aniz, 107, 150
agrarian reform bill of,
107, 111, 151, 156-157,
190-191
Baer, Werner, 220
Barros, Adhemar de, 148
Basic Reforms, Program of,
82-83, 133, 139, 198
Borges, Thomas Pompeu Accioli,
55
bossa nova, 136-137, 141, 175
See also National Demo-
cratic Union
Brazilian Communist Party (PCB),

41-42, 47
and rural labor organiza-
tion, 42, 47
Brazilian Institute of Agrarian Development, 204,
207, 217, 218
Brazilian Institute of Agrarian Reform, 102, 204,
206, 209, 217, 218, 223
Brazilian Labor Party, 81,
96, 140-155 passim,
150, 152
Goulart, 78, 80, 91, 110,
125, 138, 191, 203
origins of, 29, 124
voting behavior on Goulart
amendment and, 184,
185, 187-188, 190-191
Brazilian Rural Confederation,
27, 45, 47-48, 49-51, 85,
108
Brazilian Rural Society, 49
Brizola, Leonel, 43, 68, 81,
83, 90, 92, 95, 134, 138,
143
Bulhões, Octávio, 106
Bureaucracy
as organ of social con-
trol, 20
in the Cartorial State,
23-24
patrimonial, 16-17

Cabo eleitoral, 29

254

255

as source of authority, 32

federated interest structure in, 25

institutional crisis of, 77

Vargas and development of, 201

See also Syndicalism

Coroneis (Coronelismo), 22, 26, 28-29, 167, 176, 202

Costa e Silva, Arthur, 54, 109

Cunha, Bocayuva, 151, 153

Dantas, Santiago, 87, 91

Declaration of Goiânia, 85

Delfim Neto, Antônio, 53, 109

Democratic Parliamentary Coalition, (ADP) 81

Dos Prazares, José, 41

Economic Development (modernization)

and cartorialism, 24-25

and import substitution policy, 31-32, 220

land reform issue in, 34-39, 48, 57

military governments and, 101-103, 105-106, 198, 207, 214, 219-224, 227-230

of agrarian sector, 17, 32, 34, 39, 205

Vargas and, 23-27, 31

Electoral system, 28-32

and mass mobilization, 120, 125

coalitions in, 175

elite strategy in, 32

regional bias of, 167

under Empire, 21

under Second Republic, 28-29, 34

See also Clientelism, Populism

Elites

and interest group effectiveness, 200

and policy process, 198-200, 226-227

during revolutionary period, 215

political control by, 98, 227

Estado Nôvo, 26-28

Executive Group for Agrarian Reform, 217-218

Expropriation, 67-68, 73, 85-90 passim, 131, 135, 142

Castelo and, 206-211

Goulart decree on, 98, 140-153, 186-190, 154

in Rio Grande do Sul, 92

Institutional Act No.9 and, 215-216

Since 166, 223

256

257

in 1964 crisis, 227

linha dura of, 56, 212-214,
217

Milton Campos Commission, See
Special Commission for
Agrarian Reform

Moderating power, 16-20, 200
See also Patrimonialism

National Council on Agrarian
Reform, 86

National Democratic Union
and Castelo, 109-112,
158-159, 188
and Goulart, 78, 80,
135-136, 188
attitudes toward land
reform, 135-137, 141,
147-148, 156, 181, 184,
205
description of, 122, 175
distribution of seats in
Congress, 125
origins, 29

National Institute for Colonization and Land Reform,
219, 221

National Liberation Front, 81

Neves, Tancredo, 86, 141, 151

Parliamentary regime, 51, 64
fn., 77, 135
limitations of, 133
plebiscite on, 80, 82, 86

Patrimonialism
and planter class, 53
continuity of, 225, 228
political parties and,
124
relationship of agrarian
issue to, 34, 39
revival by Vargas of,
39-40
role of bureaucracy in,
16, 20

Peasants, See Camponeses

Peixoto, Amaral, 109-110,
137-138, 143

Pinheiro Neto, João, 94, 97,
190

Pinto, Carvalho, 83, 91

Pinto, José de Magelhaes,
135-136

Policy process
and institutional crisis,
77
Castelo strategy and,
197, 203-214
Goulart strategy and,
197-203
impact of patrimonialism,
corporatism on, 31-32
political parties participation in, 192
president and, 6-9, 52
under revolutionary
government, 100
under Second Republic, 28

Populism

    and effect on stability,
       125-127, 169

    and institutional crisis,
       77

    and agrarian reform, 40,
       92, 169, 177

    and role in electoral
       system, 31-32, 125

    and urban politics, 169,
       173-174, 177

    Goulart and, 92-94, 97,
       121, 125

    Kubitschek and, 32-34

    urban labor and, 48

Presidency

    and economic decision
       making, 6-7

    and foreign policy, 7-8

    and legislative process,
       74-76

    and policy process, 6-9,
       76, 132, 186-190,
       200-204

    crisis of authority and,
       77-78

    interest groups and, 48-51,
       128, 199-200

Program for Distribution of
    Land and Stimulus to
    Agroindustry in the North
    and Northeast (PROTERRA),221

PSD, See Social Democratic
    Party

PTB, See Brazilian Labor Party

Quadros, Jânio, 49, 77, 78,
    130, 153

Regionalism, 21-23, 84-85,
    119-120, 166-175

    municipalism as aspect of,
       83-85, 108

    See also Coroneis

Ribeiro, Paulo Assiz, 102, 107

Rodriguez, Mário Martíns, 148

Rural workers

    and Goulart land reform
       bill, 140, 207

    and revolutionary policy,
       222, 229

    Castelo consultation with,
       108

    occupational structure of,
       40, 44-45

    unionization of, 40-43, 47

Ruralist strategy, 84-85

    Also see Regionalism

Sesmarias, 18-19

    compared to Land Statute,
       207

Silva, Amaury, 47

Social Democratic Party

    and agrarian reform,
       137-138, 141-143,
       145-153, 184, 186, 205

    and Castelo, 109-110,